The
Magic and Making of
Driftwood Sculptures

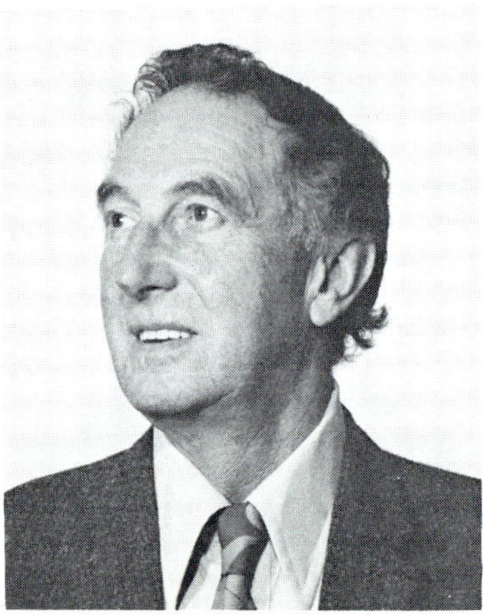

Robert Lumb studied at the Leeds College of Art, but his studies there were interrupted by the Second World War, which he spent with the Royal Navy. Later, during a busy commercial career, he built his own boat, and it was from inland waterways that he first acquired an interest in driftwood – he had to clear bits from the propellers. Forced into early semi-retirement, he came to Devon twelve years ago and now lives in Torquay. It is from the beaches of Lyme Bay and South Devon that most of his driftwood has been collected. Driftwood sculpture has pride of place among his many interests, which include photography, music, painting and sailing.

The Magic and Making of Driftwood Sculptures

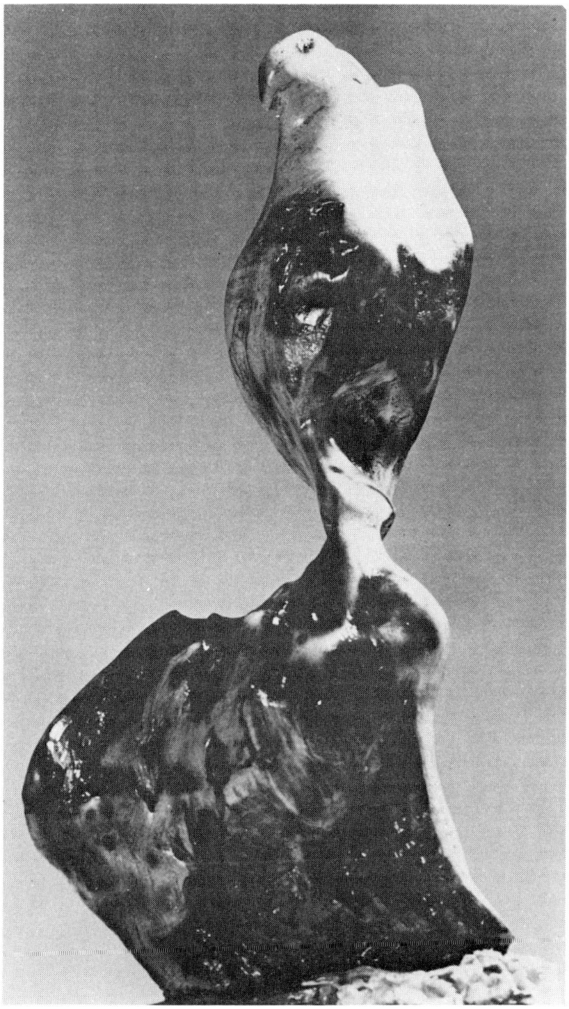

ROBERT LUMB

MIDAS BOOKS

To my wife Marian
and my dog Kim
the best driftwood collectors

In the same illustrated series

Photo Montage by Lee Campion
Shell Designs by Christine Haragan
Pressed Flower Craft by Joyce Fenton
Coal Hole Rubbings by Lily Goddard
Seed Collage by Jo Ragbourne

First published in 1983 by Midas Books
12 Dene Way, Speldhurst
Tunbridge Wells, Kent TN3 0NX

ISBN 0 85936 205 1

Designed by Joe Spark

Edited by Candida Hunt

Production for the publisher by
Chambers Green Ltd, Tunbridge Wells, Kent

Printed and bound in England

Contents

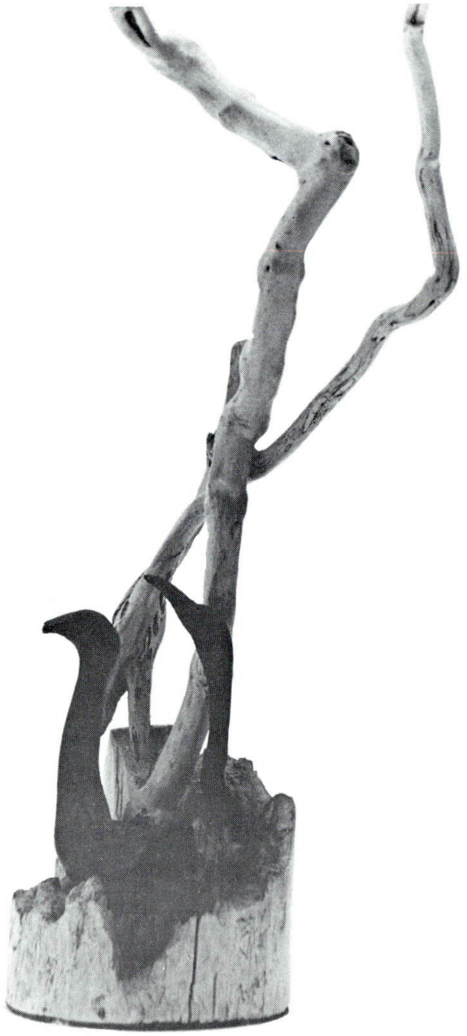

1 *'Two Birds Nesting': see plate 22 for details about how the sculpture was made.*

Introduction

This book is about natural things: the wonderful shapes and forms wrought in wood by the natural forces of our planet. They are all around us, yet how few people even notice, let alone really see them.

Driftwood is a product of nature made without interference from man. Sometimes it can be found in exquisite pieces, already fashioned and smoothed by the elements, just waiting to be taken home and mounted. More often it appears rough, deformed and seemingly not worth a second glance.

This is the challenge of driftwood sculpture. Beneath such a rugged, unimposing exterior lie undreamed-of colours, shapes and textures, intriguing in their endless variety. No two pieces are ever alike. Original and unique, much of their beauty lies hidden, just waiting to be revealed. The basic shape has already been set by nature – your hand and your imagination will do the rest. As you handle driftwood and begin to work with it the shapes guide your hand, ideas germinate and grow and you begin to discover there is magic in this medium.

People react to driftwood, and even more so to a driftwood sculpture. They like to pick it up, to feel it with their hands and explore it with their eyes. It is suggestive, it stirs the imagination and is filled with haunting moods and emotions. It can be an action piece alive with movement or possess a calm and serene tranquillity. Discovering driftwood is like finding a hidden door through which you can escape from the mad modern world; here is a quiet, creative niche that you can make all your own.

To start making driftwood sculptures you need very little. A pocket knife and a piece of sandpaper will set you on the way. In these days of expensive sports and pastimes it is rare indeed to find such an absorbing interest where the outlay is so insignificant and your raw materials are actually free. Collecting driftwood is like a treasure hunt: you never know what you are going to find. It also provides healthy outdoor fun for family and friends.

Search the strand-line of an ocean beach. Hunt in the nooks and crannies of some sandy cove. Follow the course of a rippling stream or winding river. Seek along the shoreline of a tranquil lake. Not only will you find driftwood for sculpting, you will also discover much more about the wonders of nature and your life will be the richer.

1 *The driftwood story*

There could be no driftwood without trees, so the story quite naturally begins with them. They were growing on the earth long before man appeared and their fossil remains have been traced back over three hundred million years. They are one of the most varied and widely distributed forms of plant life on our planet.

Primitive man observed the cycle of the seasons. He saw how trees came to life in the spring with young leaves and blossom. Their fruits, nuts and berries provided him with food. In winter they appeared to die but still gave him shelter and fuel. It is not surprising, therefore, that trees became part of myth, legend and religion. Some were thought to be the home of good fairies and gods, while others were reputed to be the hiding places for devils and witches. Even sober-minded ancient philosophers like Aristotle and Plutarch expressed the view that trees had perception, passion and reason.

Down through the centuries the tree beliefs of man were woven into the fabric of folklore the world over. They still retain a place in almost every modern cult and religion. One cannot think of Jesus without thinking of the wooden cross and the crown of thorns, or of Noah without the Ark. From time immemorial there have been stories rooted in the strong connections between the lives of humans and those of trees. A man's life could depend upon a tree. He could suffer if it was damaged, die slowly when it withered, or perish when it fell down.

From Ancient Egypt comes the tale of two brothers who lived three thousand years ago. One of them had to make a long journey, and being sad at leaving he hid a token of his heart among the flowers of an acacia tree so that it could be happy while he was away. Not knowing this, one day the other brother cut down the tree; at the very moment that it hit the ground the first brother in the far country fell down and died.

A superstition still persists that a person's illness can be transferred to a tree by fixing part of the sufferer's skin, hair or clothing to it. Another belief says that if a newborn male child spends his first night on earth at the foot of a sturdy oak, then he too will grow up sturdy and strong. There are many such tales of this mysterious link between trees and human life. But then, they do provide his first resting place, the cradle, and his last one, the coffin.

This bond is stronger today than it has ever been. People depict their ancestry as a 'family tree', and the bigger it is the better they like it. Trees are planted to commemorate all kinds of special events and great occasions, and though their metal tags grow green and grey they will tell our children's children who came down the road and passed this way. Trees are symbols of permanence, the essence of life and longevity; they mark the beginning and the end of an era. Some are the largest and oldest living things on earth; giant redwoods, whispering saplings when Christ was also young, are still standing today.

Children love to climb trees. Later, as courting couples they symbolize their enduring love for each other by carving their initials on some smooth and massive trunk. They leave behind them two hearts joined by an arrow. Strangely, the higher up they manage to do this the stronger, they believe, their personal bond will be.

For stirring the emotions trees have few equals. The sense of peace and tranquillity becomes almost a tangible thing when the busy city dweller escapes into the summer stillness of some woodland glade. To be alone and one with nature, to contemplate the beauty of wooded hills and quiet waters can be sheer magic, like standing on the threshold of a wonderful new life. But picture the same place on a dark, cold and stormy night when the wind is howling through the trees, when lightning strikes and thunder cracks and trees come crashing down. On such a night the imagination still hears demons shrieking and danger is not far away.

Yet both these extremes, the calm and beautiful, the angry and the wild, are the birthplace of driftwood, and it carries these characteristics with it. Long after it ceases to be a tree it still retains the beauty and serene tranquillity of those distant summers. You will also find mysterious twisted shapes that echo the darkness and power of long-forgotten storms.

Driftwood will never cease to fascinate the human race because it too is part of its story.

2 Genesis

A tremendous amount of wood finds its way into the sea. Large branches and whole trees are washed down from lakes and rivers, but driftwood does not have to be part of a tree in its natural state. It can be formed from prepared timber of every description; wooden boats, masts and spars, beach chairs, seaside chalets – in fact anything, from barges to boxes, may be swept away by gales. Ships wrecked on rocky shores break up, and their furniture and fittings eventually float free. Sooner or later almost any kind of wooden object can be found floating around in the sea. Even though these things are manmade, he takes no part in their metamorphosis into driftwood. This is the work of nature.

First there are the mighty sledgehammers, the great heaving, pounding seas that, lashed by furious winds, smash the timbers into a myriad random shapes against the rocky coasts. Shapes that are not like the preconceived ideas of a sculptor, but are wild and completely abstract. Here, being fashioned with such awesome power, are strange forms which will arouse the curiosity and excite the imagination.

A characteristic of wood is that it splits down the length of its grain and fractures across it. Whichever way it breaks in the fury of the sea, the hidden beauty starts to be revealed. At this stage it may take a fair amount of imagination to see it. Long, sharp, dangerous-looking jagged splinters may be much more apparent, but shingle, sand and surf will take care of this. As wood soaks up water it softens and becomes progressively less likely to split and fracture, and the jagged spikes become rounded by the constant rolling up and down the beach in the surf. When trunks and branches begin to lose their bark the underlying surfaces, exposed to the endless tidal action, can become very smooth indeed.

With the action of sea, sand and sun colour changes take place. Some pieces bleach to a creamy white, others, because of tree-type, resin content, grain and density, will reveal richer tones, ranging from blacks, reds and browns to softer shades of honey and amber.

Later in the book the chapter on finishes will show how these colours can be preserved by glazing. However, before you take a hand the sea still has much more to do.

Nature's workmen

As soon as floating timber begins to soften with the water it becomes

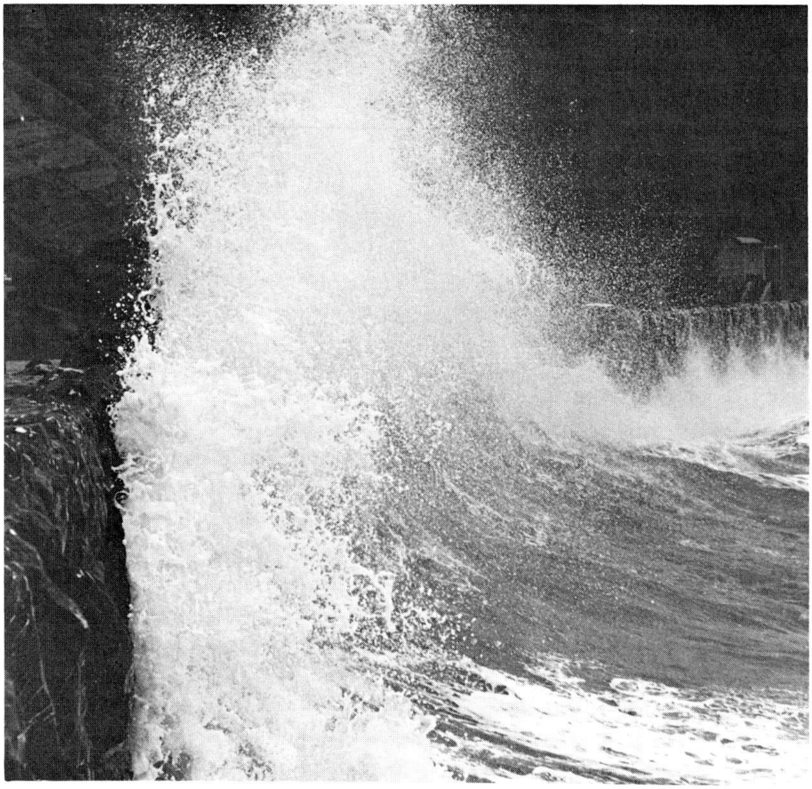

2 *These pounding seas are nature's mighty sledgehammers. Out of the fury and destruction are born the strange, random shapes of driftwood which carry their hallmark forever. After this storm there will be some interesting finds.*

a target for many forms of marine life. There are small creatures which hide in its nooks and crannies to escape from predators. Some bore holes in it to make themselves a permanent home; to others it is both a home and a source of food. Long before it becomes waterlogged and sinks, a whole army of nature's workmen are busy making the intriguing shapes and textures of driftwood.

Of particular interest are the wood borers, of which there are many; three common varieties are mentioned here.

The Wood Piddock (*Xylophaga dorsalis*) This is not a very big fellow, only about 25mm long. It makes itself a home in submerged and floating timbers by burrowing shallow, round holes about the diameter of a thin pencil. This naturally lets in more water and hastens the waterlogging process, which is fine unless it happens to be in the bottom of your boat.

The Shipworm Perhaps the best known and most feared wood borer is the Shipworm (*Terrido navalis*). This is a real terror which has been dreaded by mariners through the ages. It is not really a worm at all but a bivalve mollusc which can grow to 155mm in length (some species of *Terrido* can be double this). Not only does it bore deep holes in wooden ships but it also feeds partly on some of the timber borings as well. Its voracious appetite wrought havoc among the fleets of the ancient world. It destroyed Roman galleys, riddled the quinqueremes of Nineveh and was the scourge of the Viking longboats; but it does help to make very interesting driftwood.

The Gribble One of the most effective sea sculptors is the tiny Gribble Worm (*Limnoria lignorum*), again not a true worm but a small crustacean, only about 5mm long. Tunnelling endlessly in vast numbers, it causes submerged timber to take on a wonderful honeycomb texture. This is not, however, restricted to the geometrical symmetry of bees' combs. Perhaps a better description would be 'gribble-combed' or 'gribbled'; an example of their fine work is shown in plate 3.

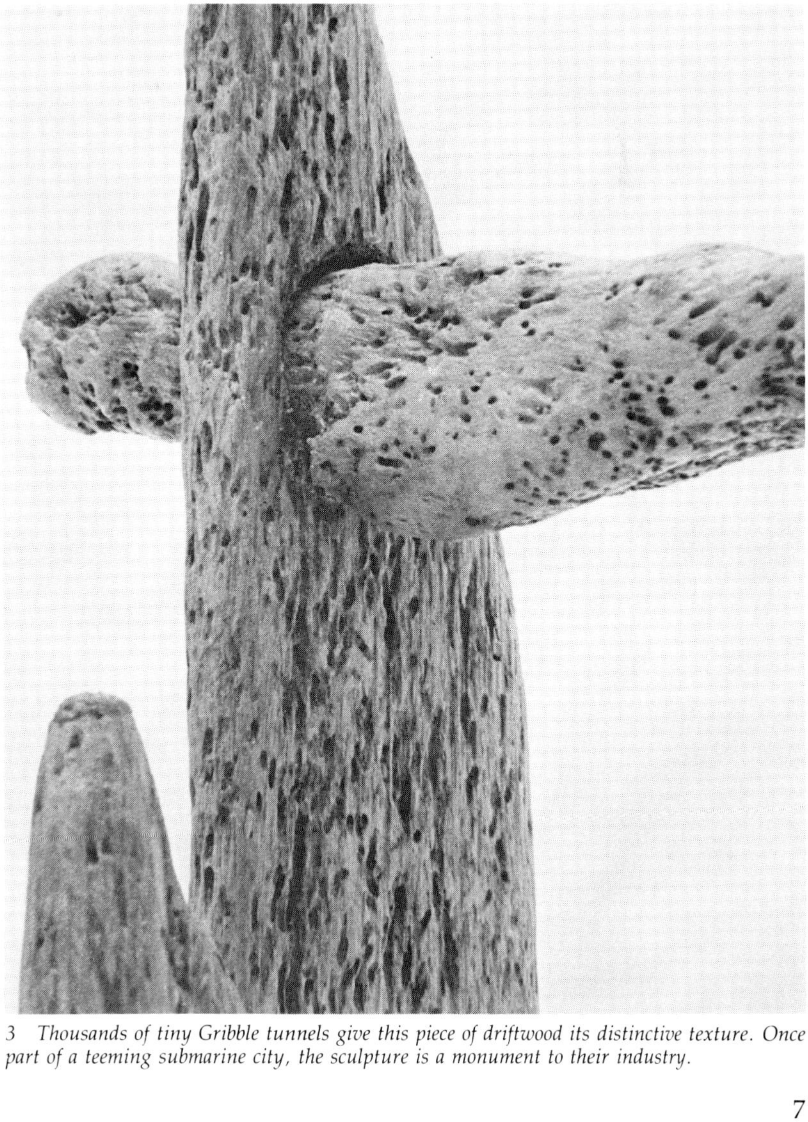

3 Thousands of tiny Gribble tunnels give this piece of driftwood its distinctive texture. Once part of a teeming submarine city, the sculpture is a monument to their industry.

The illustration shows what was probably just a length of sawn and planed timber when it originally found its way into the sea. Fortunately the Gribble does not appear to have any preferences, and you are just as likely to find a beautifully 'gribbled' log or branch when hunting along the strand-line. Occasionally you may find a piece which has been in the sea for years; such pieces are completely covered with countless thousands of tiny holes so that the surface takes on a crusty, almost fossilized, appearance. An extra bonus would be to find that barnacles had also colonized the wood; this additional encrustation can make driftwood have the look and feel of a piece from a petrified forest.

Good driftwood for sculpting is old and well seasoned. Its character is forged slowly by many natural processes. It is not always easy to find, but then the best things seldom are.

3 Finding the raw materials

Collecting driftwood can be a very pleasant occupation. It can occupy a quiet hour on a peaceful stroll, or be an energetic family picnic that lasts all day. It can be great fun for everyone concerned, and most remarkable of all, here is something useful which is still free for the finding. You can leave the finding of it to random chance, but knowing where and when to look can make an excursion all the more rewarding. If you cannot get to the coast then rivers, reservoirs and lakes will be your hunting grounds. Access to many of these areas is now open to the public, but remember to respect the rights of farmers and landowners and do not trespass.

Lakes

Mountain lakes and reservoirs surrounded by barren hills and moors are not the best places to find driftwood unless they are fed by rivers and streams which flow through woodland areas. To find out what a stretch of water might have to offer, first look at the geographical detail of the surrounding areas; do not assume that the shores will be fringed with masses of driftwood just waiting for you to fish it out. It does not work that way.

Very often a lake will have its own prevailing wind direction caused by the height and location of adjacent hills. The wind being funnelled across the surface through the valleys will blow driftwood onto the opposite shore. Rivers and streams which feed the lake will set up currents in the water. Where these deposit their driftwood will depend not only upon the strength of the flow but also on the nature of the lake bed. Although the surface is flat, beneath it there may be submerged hills and valleys. (This would be indicated if there were islands in the lake.)

The fact that driftwood may be waterlogged and partly rotten does not mean that it is useless. In most pieces there is a skeleton structure of harder wood. As an example of this, think of the knots that can be seen in cut and sawn timber; anyone who has tried to put a screw into a knot knows how hard it is to penetrate. For the purpose of driftwood sculpture regard rotten wood as only the soft 'flesh' which has to be removed. The resulting 'bones' beneath often reveal the most exciting shapes – but more about this later.

The changing strand-lines

In an average year water levels are higher in winter than they are in summer. Winter gales are more prolonged and severe, and this is the time when most timber gets into the water. It is important to remember this because the winter strand-line will be on higher ground. How much higher depends on how steeply the lake bed shelves and the extent to which it may flood. A lake with gentle shallows may have a winter strand-line many yards back from where you may be hopefully scouring the water's edge on a hot summer's day. A further point to bear in mind is that driftwood which was stranded there may well be hidden in a seasonal growth of long grasses.

Rivers

After heavy rains rivers rise rapidly, some perhaps three metres or more in a single day. Apart from being very impressive they pick up and transport a tremendous amount of debris in their rushing waters. As they scour and burst their banks great quantities of earth get washed away, and the roots of what appeared to be firmly anchored big trees lose their hold. They topple into the raging torrent and begin their journey into driftwood.

The foolhardy, foraging among very powerful and dangerous

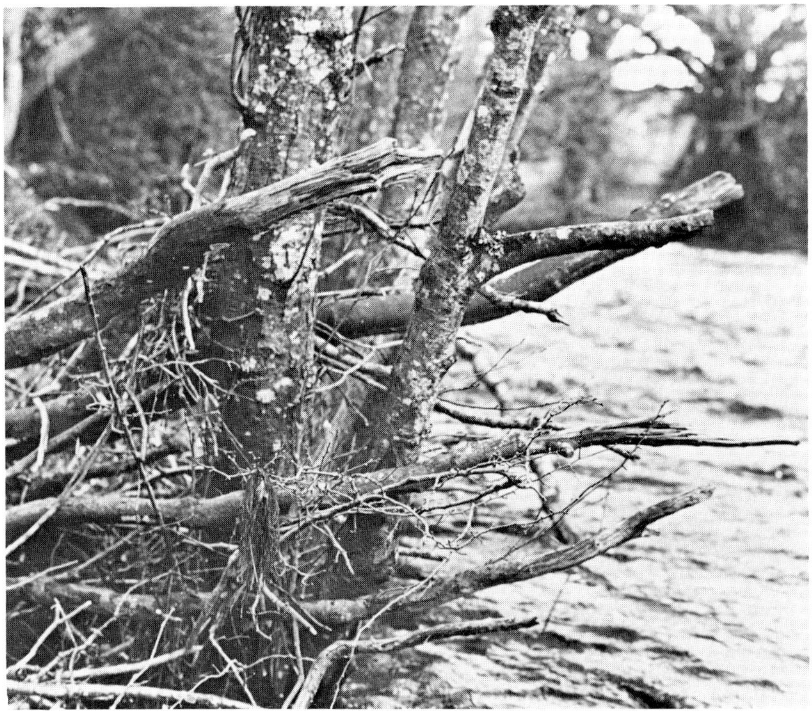

4 Driftwood in the making. This tangle of debris testifies to the height and fury of recent flood waters. At this stage the wood is too new and green and has not yet developed the essential weathered characteristics of mature driftwood. Future storms will wash some of it back into the river to continue its journey into driftwood.

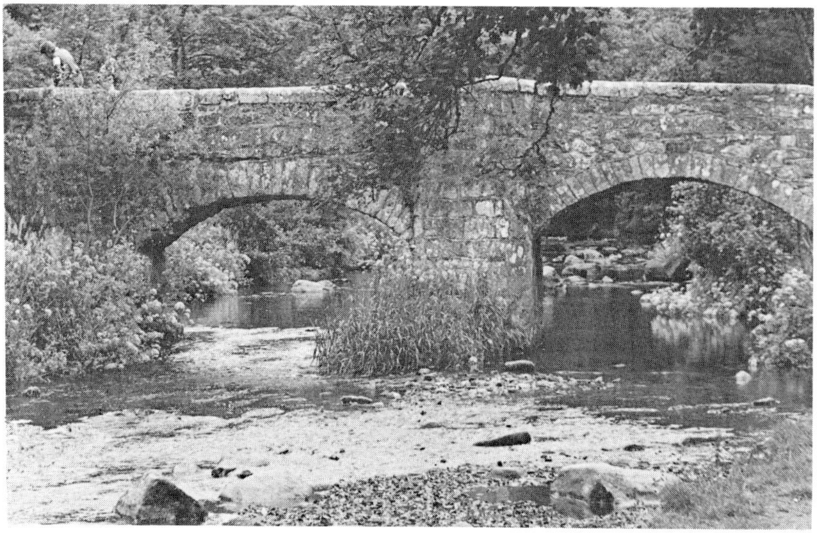

5 What other hobby provides free raw materials from such idyllic surroundings and gives so much pleasure in the finding? Seek out the quiet places, fill your soul full of peace and your bag full of driftwood.

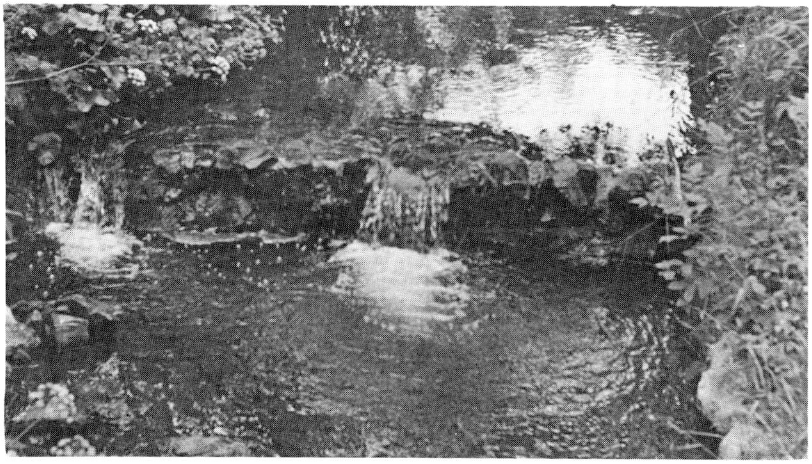

6 Driftwood is where you find it. This quiet stream is a good hunting ground; pieces of hard wood may have been trapped here for a long time, being fashioned and mellowed with the years. Remember to look on the banks among the summer foliage which hides the higher winter strand-line.

currents, will certainly find plenty of fresh floating timber, but it is not much use for driftwood sculpture. It is still raw and green, immature and devoid of character; taking it at this stage is almost akin to sacrilege, as you deprive it forever of its potential – the beauty of its maturity is lost for all time.

When the river has subsided then is good hunting at hand. The force of the water will have dislodged many useful pieces of much older driftwood which have long been exposed to the hand of nature: pieces that became wedged among rocks, held fast by tree roots, trapped in underwater caves and in all manner of places where water continued to flow over them. Or perhaps they were abandoned in some quiet backwater as the river gently receded in a summer's drought. Such pieces will already have acquired the character and shapes which will eventually bring so much pleasure to you and all who come into contact with your creations.

Where do you find these pieces? A good place to start looking is where the river bends. The outer edge of a bend usually has the stronger current and deeper water; the inner side of the bend is more likely to have shallows and a strand-line. Where tree branches overhang and dip into the water a possible catchment area is formed. If the river has been very high useful material may be lodged in the lower branches.

Weirs and rapids

Weirs and rapids are good places to look, but beware of wet and slippery footholds. Here the speed of the water increases, and driftwood which has been idling in the eddies gets drawn back into the main current. The sudden shallowing of the water frequently strands ideal pieces and the sheer volume and force of the water flowing over them has a wonderful smoothing action.

Other places where driftwood gets stranded are against the pillars of a bridge or the piles of a jetty. Low-lying water-meadows frequently get inundated and are well worth a visit. On navigable rivers and canals there are locks, quays and docks to investigate; when exploring on a river bank remember to check out those favourite 'fishing holes', as many a fine piece of driftwood is hooked by anglers and then cast aside by the water's edge.

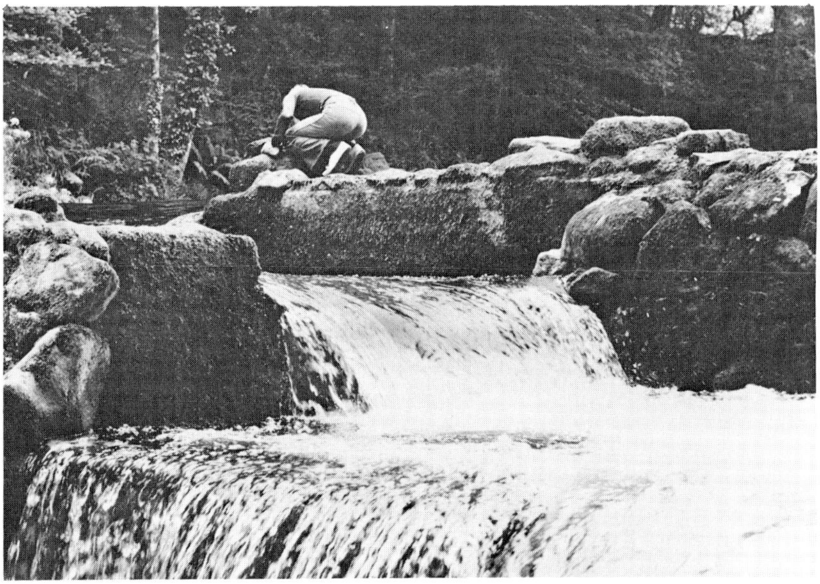

7 Trapped in a perpetual swirl of water, driftwood is smoothed and polished. Eventually it will move downstream on its journey to the sea. It may look like rubbish now, but just you wait.

The sea

There can be no doubt that the sea is the greatest provider of materials for the driftwood sculptor. Almost any beach will provide driftwood at one time or another. By giving some thought to where and when to look for it, some of the elements of random chance can be eliminated.

Local knowledge If you live near the sea then you may already have some knowledge of the coast. Should you not be so fortunate there are plenty of people you can turn to for advice. Consult the local seafarers, the fishermen, boatmen, ferrymen and yachtsmen. Their safety at sea depends on their knowledge of tides, currents and prevailing winds in the area. They would probably be delighted to suggest places where you could start your search.

Beachcombing has always been a way of life for a few who live near the sea, and with the advent of modern metal detectors beachcoming has graduated to treasure hunting. The enthusiasts who use these are intent on finding pieces of eight and Spanish doubloons. Very few of them will take driftwood, but they can still tell you where it is.

If you enjoy talking to the local people a casual word in pub or hotel bar could be both rewarding and entertaining. When it becomes known you are a driftwood sculptor, curiosity is aroused. People react to driftwood, and showing a photograph or two of your work could have surprising results. You may be sure of plenty of advice, and perhaps even a commission.

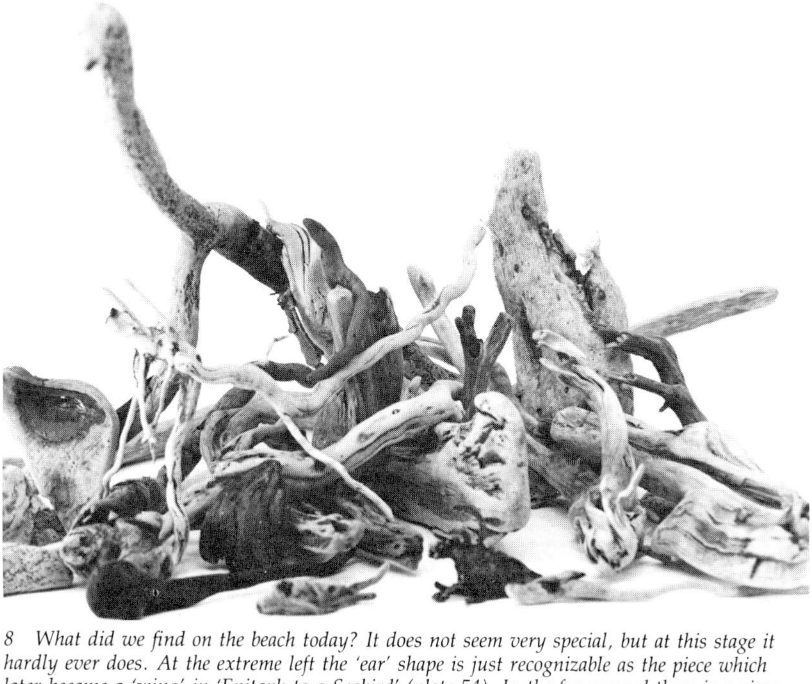

8 What did we find on the beach today? It does not seem very special, but at this stage it hardly ever does. At the extreme left the 'ear' shape is just recognizable as the piece which later became a 'wing' in 'Epitaph to a Seabird' (plate 54). In the foreground there is a piece which deserves closer scrutiny (see plate 9).

Beach strand-lines Just as rivers and lakes have their own particular ways of stranding driftwood, so too does the sea. As waves roll up the beach on an incoming tide their forward motion is stronger than the backwash. This forward speed and strength can be clearly seen in the way surfboard riders come ashore on the crest of a wave. Less spectacularly, most of the debris carried by the waves is eventually left behind on the strand-line or high-water mark, which is of course one of the main places to look for driftwood.

On the rocky beaches the strand-line is less easy to define than it is on sand or shingle. The rocks themselves will make barriers to, or traps for, driftwood coming ashore, so be prepared to search a wider area. The best finds are usually made after a good strong gale with the winds blowing onto the land.

Check the tides Although it is not possible to predict gales very far ahead you can time your expeditions to coincide with the spring tides, which are the most favourable ones. These have nothing to do with the season of spring, but relate to the heights of tides and give the highest high-water marks and the lowest low-waters. They occur at full and new moon, which is approximately every two weeks. Spring tides are caused by the combined gravitational pull of the sun and the moon when both are in direct line with the earth. In calm weather exploring the edge of a very low tide may produce some unusual pieces of

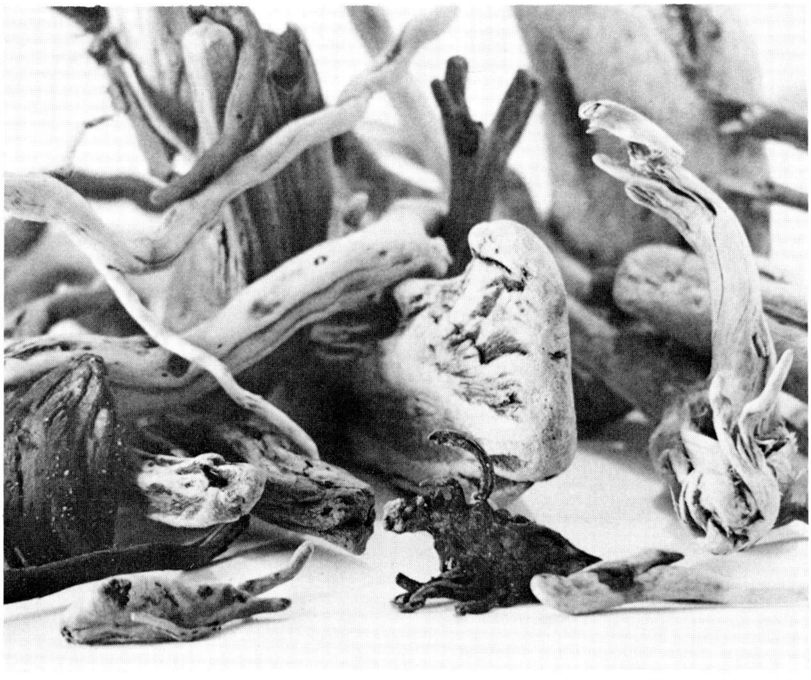

9 Here in more detail is the front row, with quite an unusual stranger sitting in the middle. He's a bit on the small side, but with driftwood big is not always best. It looks like a ready-made something, but what? See plate 10.

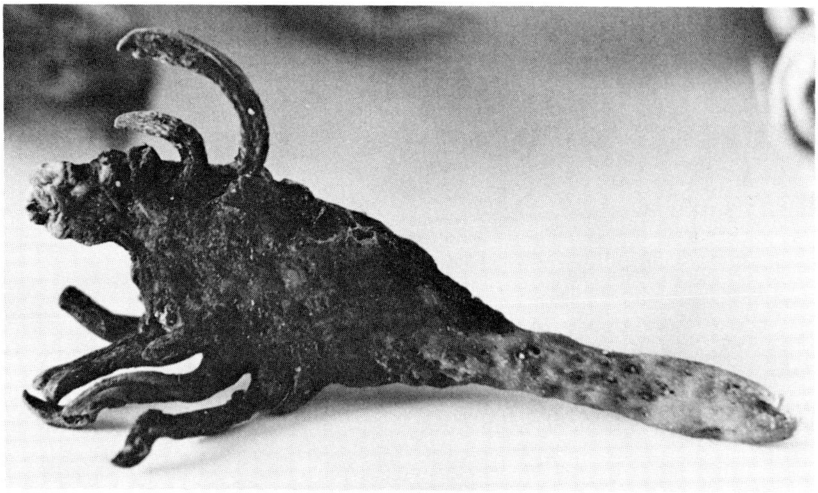

10 Now you can see the little stranger more clearly. If you cannot put a name to it do not worry, at this stage nor could anyone else. This is the sort of 'creature' that makes driftwood sculpture so intriguing and original. Clean it up and give it a dry home, and one day you will find the right niche for it. It may help you to create a mythical beast, or excite interest by peeping from a hole or shell in part of your work.

driftwood which, having long since lost their buoyancy, may have been on the sea bed for years.

Tide-tables giving the time and height of the tides are availabe in shipping manuals. Many holiday areas have small abridged local tables. These cost only a few pence and can be obtained in local booksellers, yacht chandlers and fishing tackle shops. It is important to know what the tide is doing to avoid the danger of being cut off by the sea coming in behind you and finding too late that you cannot retrace your steps. Timing collecting expeditions to just after high water could be prudent on a strange beach.

What to look for

If you approach a beach from a high vantage point you could get a grandstand view of the strand-line. This is a good place to pause and make a mental fix of anything which looks interesting. Down at beach level there is a tendency to keep your eyes down and follow your nose.

When going out to collect your material take a convenient bag to put it in and a small pocketknife. Use this to probe soft driftwood; if you can feel hard wood beneath the surface there could well be an interesting shape just waiting to be revealed. Some of your best creations may eventually be worked from just such a piece. Cutting and scraping away soft bits is usually easy to do and can produce some surprising results. The sculpture 'Penguinity' (plate 19) is just such an example: the spaces between the figures were originally soft wood which was removed with a pocketknife.

There are no rules about what to collect. It is the things which appeal to you that count. To expect to find intriguing weathered shapes ready

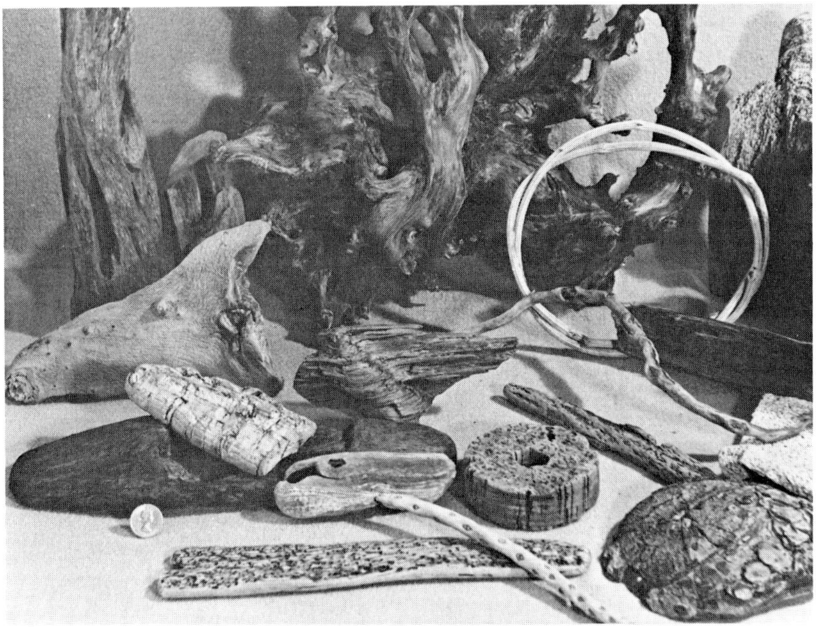

11 This may look like a construction kit, but driftwood does not come in kit form. These pieces have been cleaned and dried, and with the exception of the large piece in the background are just as they were found. At this stage it is anybody's guess what they will eventually be.

for mounting is not asking too much – it does happen, but not very often. At first the driftwood that you find may be disappointing, but after a while you will begin to notice the different patterns and colours, and in no time at all you will be seeing all kinds of fascinating shapes.

Some random pieces of driftwood are pictured in plate 11. With the exception of the larger piece in the centre background they are nothing very special to look at now, yet these are typical of the pieces from which many of the sculptures illustrated were made. Remember that the most unlikely looking material can be full of hidden secrets. So for now, if you are just beginning and have no clear idea of what you are going to make, collect any pieces which strike you as strange, unusual or curious. Driftwood is full of surprises, as you will see.

Driftwood tree roots

The upper size limit of driftwood is enormous, and those who wish to express their creative urges on the grand scale will need special equipment, like mechanical diggers, cranes, lorries and chain saws. Armed with these it would be possible to collect the multi-ton monsters which the sea, with such ease, occasionally washes ashore to confront astonished mortals.

For people with more modest ambitions smaller pieces of driftwood tree roots can provide challenging and satisfying material to work with. Root sections are more intricate and complex; but do not worry on that score, this is driftwood and in due course they will suggest to you what they want to be.

Most tree stumps and roots do not look very attractive when you find them. They may be ragged, with peeling bark and nooks and crannies filled with soft, rotting wood. Do not let this discourage you. Once you have worked with them you will be constantly amazed and gratified by what you discover.

Examples of useful root pieces are shown in plates 12 to 15.

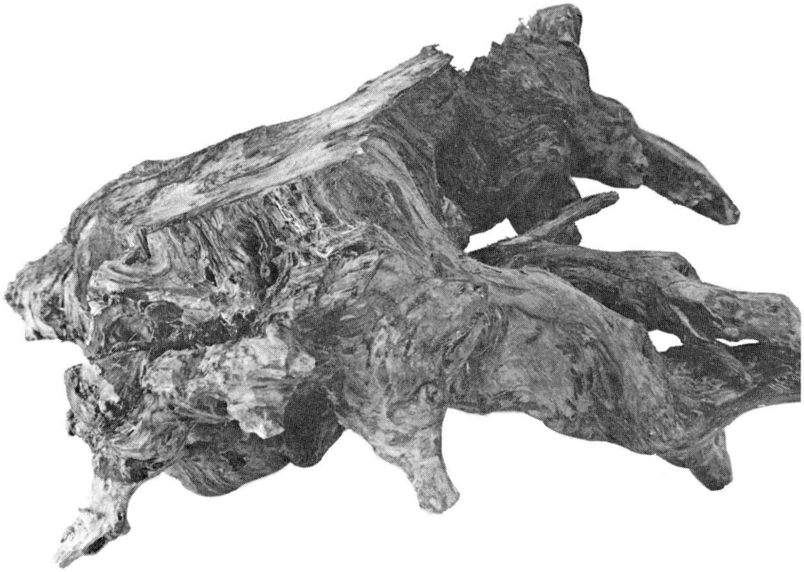

12 Not quite too big to carry home, this tree root shows good promise with many interesting shapes already being revealed. Sea and sand have left a clean and weathered surface ready for working. A find like this is guaranteed to get your imagination to work.

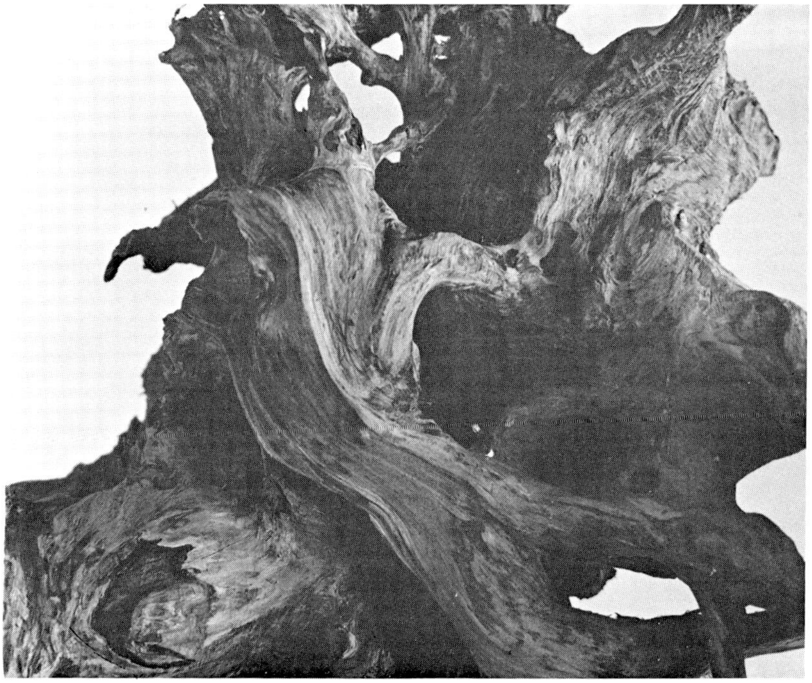

13 The underside of this tree root never saw the light of day. Now stripped bare of the earth that cloaked its growth from seedling days, its virgin beauty lies revealed to curious human gaze. Rotate the page slowly, look deeply, and you will find faces of animals, birds and men.

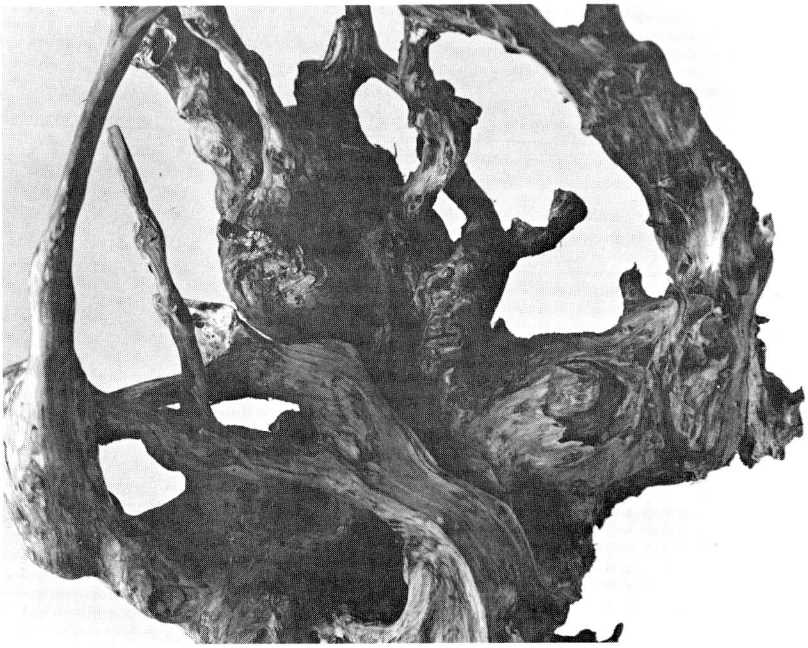

14 This is a time to let your eyes explore the beautiful shapes and your hands caress the curves, to finger the holes and feel the textures. In myth and legend holes in trees were reputed to be a hiding place of devils; holes in driftwood sculpture are always fascinating features and can lend an air of mystery to your work.

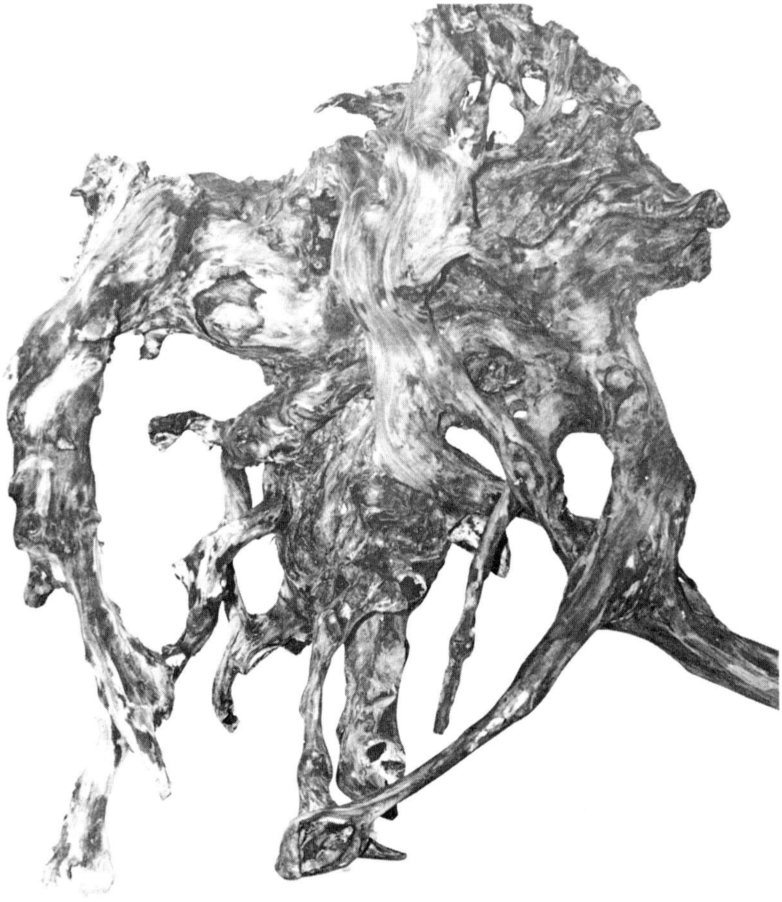

15 When you find it difficult to decide what to do next or where to make cuts, work patiently at refining what you already have. A lot of pleasurable work is still needed to smooth rough areas and clean out the holes and crevices in this piece. Always try to make curves flow gracefully into each other. With constant handling some of the driftwood magic will rub off on to you and eventually, when the time is ripe, you will know where you need to use the saw.

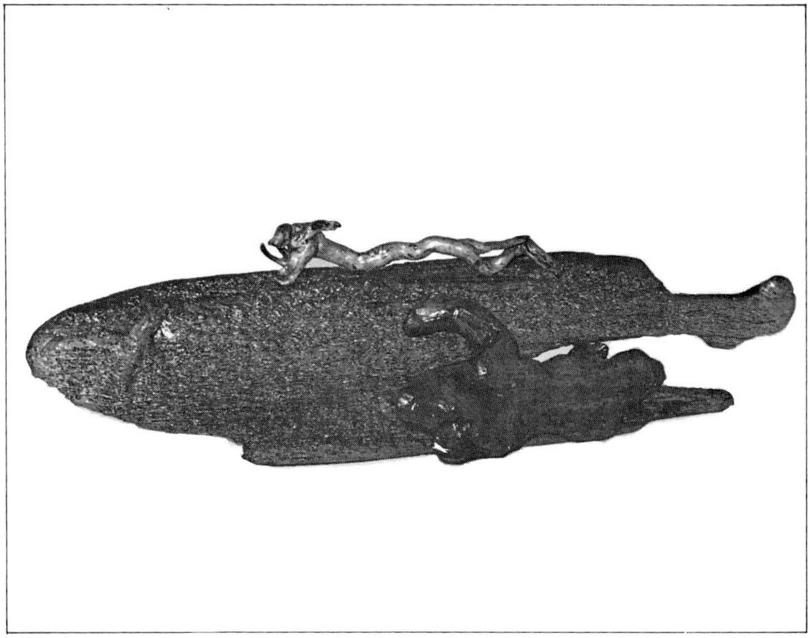

16 A small piece of driftwood used exactly as it was found is the 'mermaid' reclining on top of 'Mermaid, Fish and Frog'. The three pieces which comprise this sculpture were found close together on the same beach. The 'fish' section also required very little work; it was used because it was a naturally free-standing piece not dependent on a separate base. It was also a very fine example of the work of the Gribble. 'Frog', who completes the trio, makes this sculpture a study in three different woods and how they have each reacted to the sea. He was fashioned from a random, chunky piece of driftwood which when found had little to recommend it apart from the apparent ease with which it could be carved and the temptation to have a go.

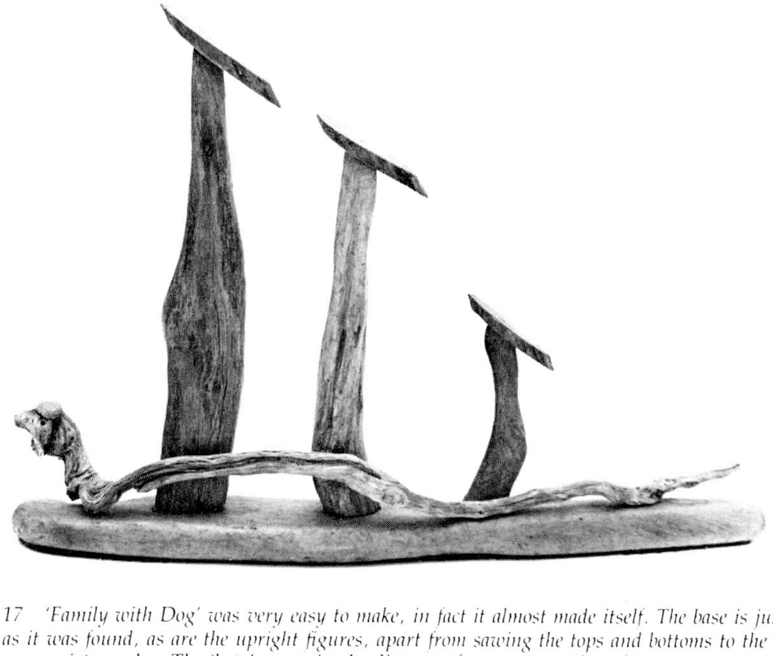

17 'Family with Dog' was very easy to make, in fact it almost made itself. The base is just as it was found, as are the upright figures, apart from sawing the tops and bottoms to the appropriate angles. The 'hats' were simply slices cut from a companion piece.

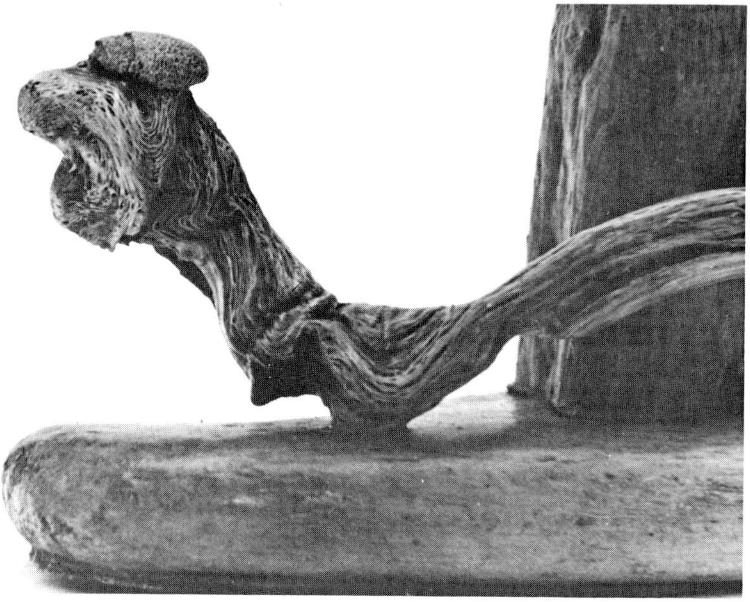

18 This photograph shows a close-up of 'Dog', who was the cause of this sculpture. He is shown here exactly as he was found. (If it bothered you that he is also wearing a hat, you could just cut it off!) The only other working for this group was to sandpaper the uprights to a smooth, professional finish, to screw the parts together and to cover the underside of the base with green felt. Waxing and buffing completed the work.

The technique of 'controlled burning' discussed in chapter 8 adds a fascinating new dimension to driftwood working and makes the job much easier.

Smaller pieces and 'Family with Dog'

Big can be beautiful, but not everyone wants to carry home a wet tree root. There is driftwood to please everybody, and at the other end of the scale there are smaller finds which can be just as surprising, and most unexpected because they could so easily have been overlooked.

When you go out collecting it is a good policy to examine even the smallest bits of driftwood because they too can have a place in the scheme of things. Plate 17 shows the sculpture 'Family with Dog'. The 'Dog' part of it, shown in more detail in plate 18, is typical of a small piece which could have been missed on the beach. Right from the start it seemed to have a dog-like face, and the long body put it straight into the dachshund category. The fact that it has no legs is artist's licence – if this bothers you then you, the creator, could make some!

The most significant part about this small dog is that it is exactly as it was found. The surface was smooth and nicely detailed, and it had a texture which was reminiscent of old ivory. There was absolutely no cutting or shaping to do at all. The only work done on it was the cementing and pinning in place once the final composition had been decided. It did, of course, have seal and glaze applied later along with the other figures in the group.

Cleaning and storing

Some of the driftwood that you collect will have been cleaned and scoured by the sea, and the sun may have obligingly bleached and dried it for you. If not, then a few simple precautions taken now will ensure that you have clean, dry materials to work with later.

Some initial pruning may have to be done, but do be sparing with a saw in the early stages. Try to restrict any cutting which has to be done to the removal of ragged, damaged and more featureless parts. This is also a time for cutting any big pieces down to a suitable size. At this stage, when you probably do not know what you are going to make or how big it will be, a suitable size is the largest piece you can comfortably handle and store.

If there are any oil or grease spots present, remove these now with white spirit or turpentine. Seaweed must be cleaned off before it starts to decay; a good scraping and a stiff brush is all that it requires. Barnacles often colonize old driftwood, but before scraping these off consider your alternatives. Their rough shells can add an extra dimension to your work: they provide a very positive contrast of texture and colour and accept glaze and varnish well. They have lived in harmony with driftwood in the sea and there is often no reason why they should not continue to do so in a driftwood sculpture. Barnacles can be cleaned by immersing or brushing with bleach diluted 1 part to 16 parts of water. Leave for about an hour and then brush and rinse well. If you get bleach on your skin rinse it off immediately.

Getting rid of sand, mud, salt and the like only needs soapy water, a drop of disinfectant and a bit of an effort. A good washing now will get you off to a better start with clean materials to work with. Now is also a good time to do a bit of peeling and scraping if there is any loose bark to be removed, as it comes off more easily when the wood is wet.

After cleaning and washing it is important to let your driftwood dry naturally and slowly in a well-ventilated place. Avoid the temptation of a quick dry near a fire or radiator; this invariably leads to disconcerting splits which can ruin a good piece.

Store driftwood in cool, dry conditions, preferably in open boxes or baskets and off the ground. If you store it in an outside garden shed and insects are a problem, dust or spray with a normal garden insecticide.

If, in a reflective mood, you should stand back and survey your new collection you may well wonder what on earth you are going to do with it now. Don't worry! Making driftwood sculptures is a wonderful exercise in free thinking. Everything will turn out fine. Very soon you will find lots of ideas – it is all part of the magic of this medium.

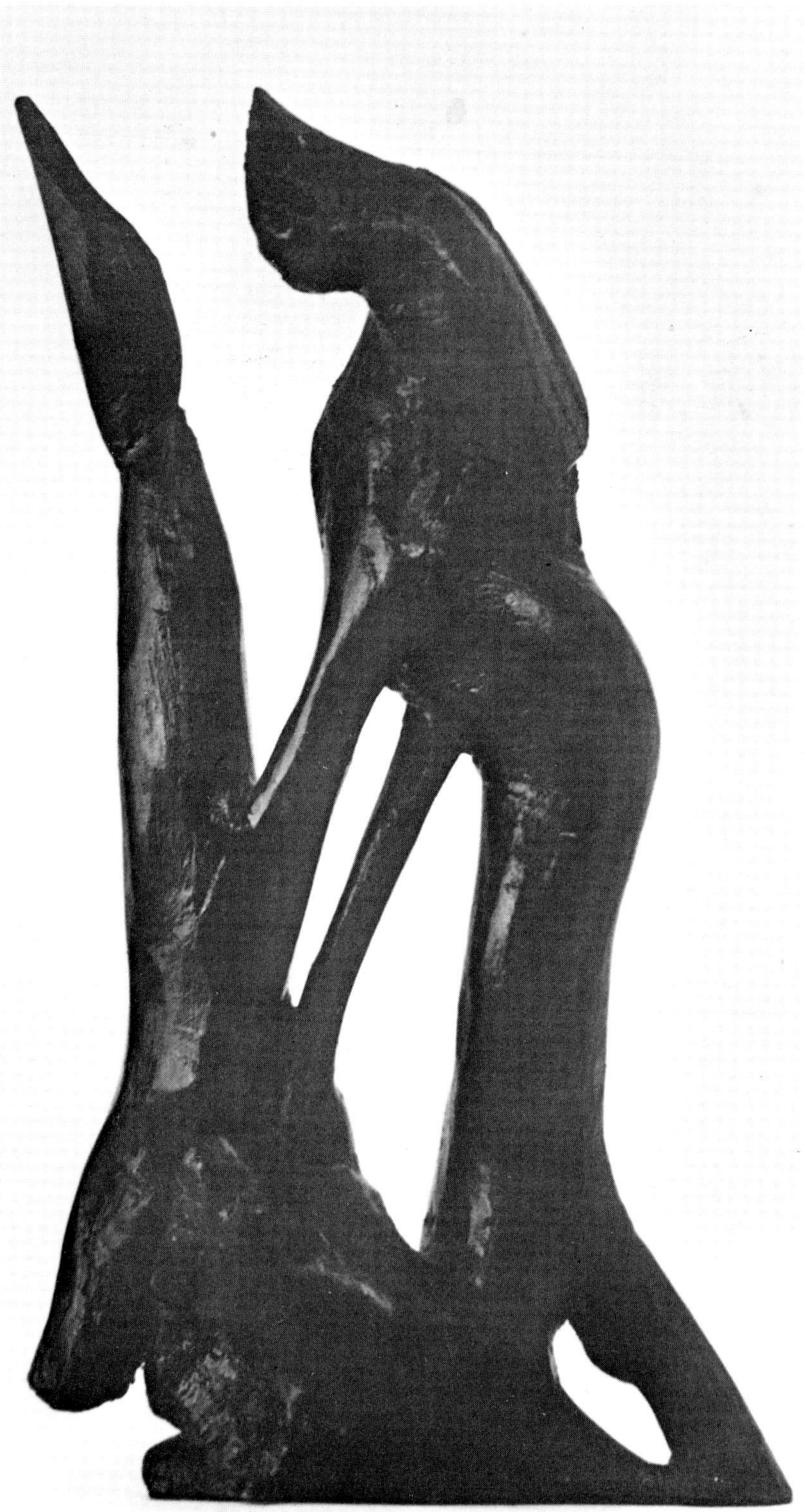

19 Almost everything about driftwood sculpture is unusual. 'Penguinity', shown here, is no exception. Its unique form was achieved by carving away soft outer wood and exploring for the hidden shapes of harder wood which lay concealed beneath. It was made with only a pocketknife and some strips of sandpaper.

4 Before you begin

Made with a pocketknife

You do not need to be a skilled carpenter or wood carver to make a start on driftwood sculpture. Nor do you need expensive tools or an elaborately equipped workshop. Patience, curiosity about driftwood and an interesting shape to clean up is enough to start you on your way with a fascinating new hobby.

Earlier in the book it was stated that a pocketknife and some sandpaper would get you started. These were the only tools used to fashion 'Ocean and Doah' (say this a bit faster and it becomes 'Oh Shenandoah', the old sea shanty). Another sculpture made in this way is 'Penguinity'. These two sculptures are illustrated in plates 19, 20 and 21.

The driftwood for these two sculptures was unusual. It was thick, old, twisted ivy. It first attracted attention because of the strange, intimate way in which the branches had grafted themselves together. This grafting can be clearly seen in the way that 'Ocean and Doah' cling together, and it was a feature which simply had to be preserved. Now, as individuals in their own right, they can dance on in their loving embrace for all eternity. It is only necessary to glance again at the illustration to see that this sculpture is alive with happiness and movement. How this or any other mood comes about is difficult to explain. There was no intention to capture this or any other feeling; with driftwood, as you will see, these things just happen. To describe how 'Ocean and Doah' began life as a sculpture it is necessary to go back to the strand-line.

The making of 'Ocean and Doah'

The pieces of ivy, still clinging to the trunk of their host tree, looked very bedraggled when they came ashore after a gale. It was only when a mass of tangled seaweed was lifted aside that the curious shapes were noticed in a piece which was as long as a man's arm and as thick as his wrist. The sea had softened it, which enabled it to be prised loose, tatty and ragged and with long strips of peeling bark. Not a bit like a present from the seaside.

The rest of the bark peeled easily with just the aid of a pocketknife. Underneath, the wood was smooth and creamy white, and just soft enough to be cut and shaped – but shaped into what? At this stage

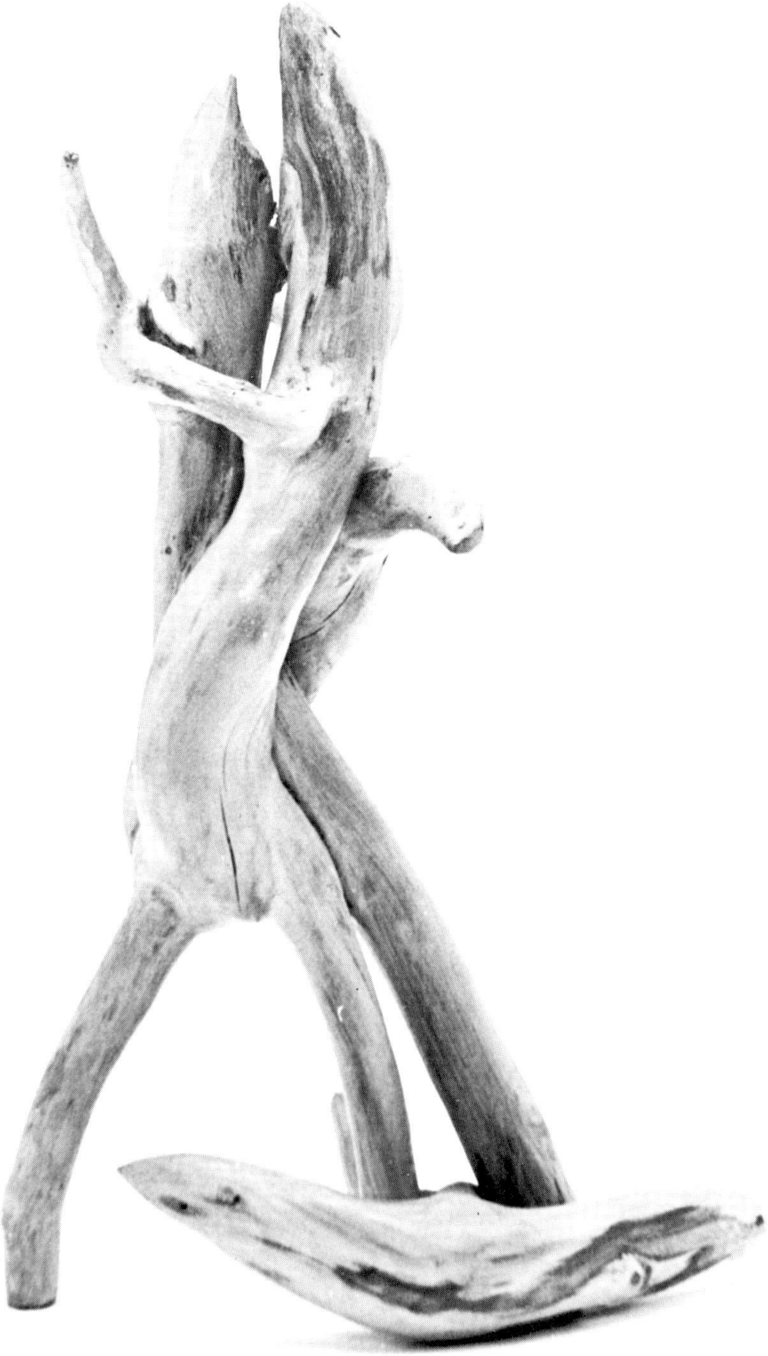

20 'Ocean and Doah'; the inseperable lovers dance on into eternity.

there was not the slightest clue to what it was going to be, and it was a case of searching for interesting and unusual features.

Trimming The knife point was used to clean out the crevices between the interwoven branches. Broken and jagged spurs were sliced off. In the more accessible places the knife blade was held at right-angles to the wood and used with a scraping action to streamline curves. Small, thin branches were removed where they seemed to impede the symmetry or flow of the others.

Isolating the action It was during this cleaning-up process that more definite shapes became apparent. The hands had been getting to know the feel of the piece; the eye had been comparing, contrasting and seeking out interesting detail and the mind was at work and bringing imagination into play. Where previously only patterns were evident, now ideas of some sort of figures in action began to form.

Where did the action seem to be strongest? There was an interesting swirl of action at one end, but which way up should it be? Did it look better in the vertical or horizontal position? The way out of this, or any other dilemma which driftwood sculpture poses, is to be aware of the questions as they come to mind and try to answer them.

Concentrating on the end where the swirling forms were most apparent, it was decided that the less interesting bits should be cut away from the opposite end. From being about one metre in length it was now reduced to less than half the size, so that the parts which in life had grafted themselves together now became the focal point.

Simplifying Two small, curved branches which encircled the grafted area now appeared to be like arms clinging to each other. Quite suddenly a likeness was seen of two people wrestling; but were they wrestling or dancing? People dancing, with three feet on the ground and two other legs sticking out behind the back of one of them? This seemed a bit far-fetched even for driftwood, so there was a long pause for thought and then finally the spare legs were cut off. This left just three feet on the ground, some with legs longer than the others. To put this right was simple: the piece was held upright against the edge of the table, a mark was made at the required length and the knife used to trim away the surplus soft wood.

Emphasizing the shapes From a meaningless jumble on the seashore to a free-standing figure! No, it was not just a lucky fluke, with driftwood this happens all the time. But there was still much to do, and with ideas crystallizing fast it was time to get on with it.

Above those embracing arms were far too many surplus branches, so these were now reduced to just the two which formed the main 'bodies'. These were then shortened, carefully leaving enough wood above the arms to allow for the shaping of heads (which at this point were still non-existent). To have carved heads with any detailed resemblance to the shape of human heads would have broken up the smooth flow of the sculpture, so tapered heads were made to emphasize the natural lines.

That is how 'Ocean and Doah' were discovered, and what happened next was quite routine. The piece was left to dry in a cool, airy place for several weeks. As it dried, the wood became much harder and more durable, and was then sandpapered to a silk-smooth finish before glazing. These aspects of finishing and mounting are covered in later sections of the book.

Other tools

So much for working with just a pocketknife, which of course is only possible with soft materials. For harder driftwood, and most of it is much harder, other tools are required. Many of these may already be in the household tool box. If not, you will not have to spend much money to get a basic kit together. Some of the most useful items are listed below.

Saws A medium-sized, general-purpose saw will cover most of your larger sawing needs. For small work a junior hacksaw or coping saw and a keyhole saw will be needed.

Pincers Driftwood may contain old nails and screws, and apart from removing these pincers are very useful for snipping away small unwanted pieces of wood. They are stronger than a pair of scissors and it saves having to fetch some secateurs from the bottom of the garden.

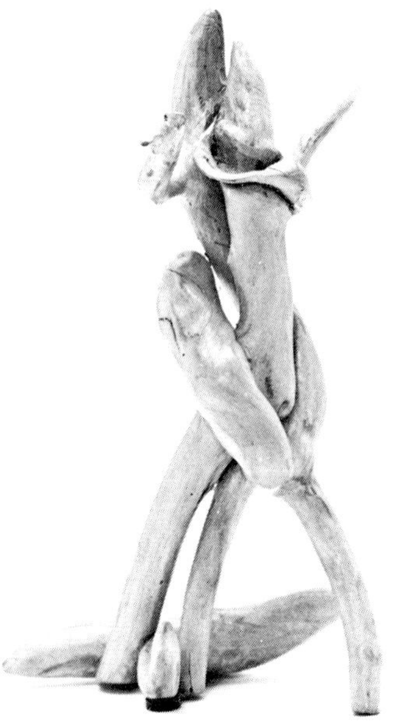

21 Another view of 'Ocean and Doah' which emphasizes their togetherness. On the living tree the branches had grafted themselves onto each other – it would have been sacrilege to part them.

Surforms These tools have taken over many of the functions of the older file-type rasps. They provide a quick method of removing surplus wood. Choose one with a flat blade for work on broad surfaces and another with a cylindrical blade for enlarging and shaping holes and curves.

Chisels From the almost infinite variety of shapes and sizes available keep your choice simple to begin with. A couple of small, flat-bladed chisels of, say 5mm and 15mm, together with a 15mm gouge (a half-rounded chisel), will be quite adequate. Add special wood-carving chisels later if you wish, but most driftwood sculptures are sufficiently compelling without the need to resort to intricate carving.

Hammer Of course this modern artifact, which was also one of early man's first weapons and tools, has to be included. You probably will not need it to bang your neighbour over the head, as he did, but it will come in mighty useful for fixing things with small panel pins; so do not choose a very big one.

Screwdriver Apart from their use with screws these tools always seem to be used for other jobs, such as levering, digging, scraping and poking, so find one with a comfortable grip and a shaft of about 15 cm with a 5 mm tip.

Drills A hand drill with a range of bit sizes is essential when it comes to fixing sculptures neatly on to prepared bases, and this is where much of the basic drill work takes place. However, if you have an electric multi-speed drill its numerous attachments offer many facilities in other ways of working, such as cutting, sawing, polishing and grinding.

This is by no means a formidable list of tools, and with these basic items you will be able to accomplish some very fine and satisfying work. Tools used for cutting and shaping should always be kept sharp; if you try to make do with blunt ones you will do less than justice to yourself.

The only other essential hardware required is an assortment of screws, nails and panel pins; to avoid future rust-staining in your sculptures always use stainless steel, brass or other non-ferrous types.

Adhesives and other materials required for finishing work are discussed in a later section.

A place to work

Although it is an advantage to have a well-equipped workshop it is by no means essential. A converted attic, basement, garage or garden shed can serve equally well. It is important to have a solid table or bench to work on. It is also necessary to have a vice or some other means of fastening and holding a piece of wood firm while you work on it. A final point is that your workshop should be dry, as you cannot get a good, smooth finish on damp driftwood.

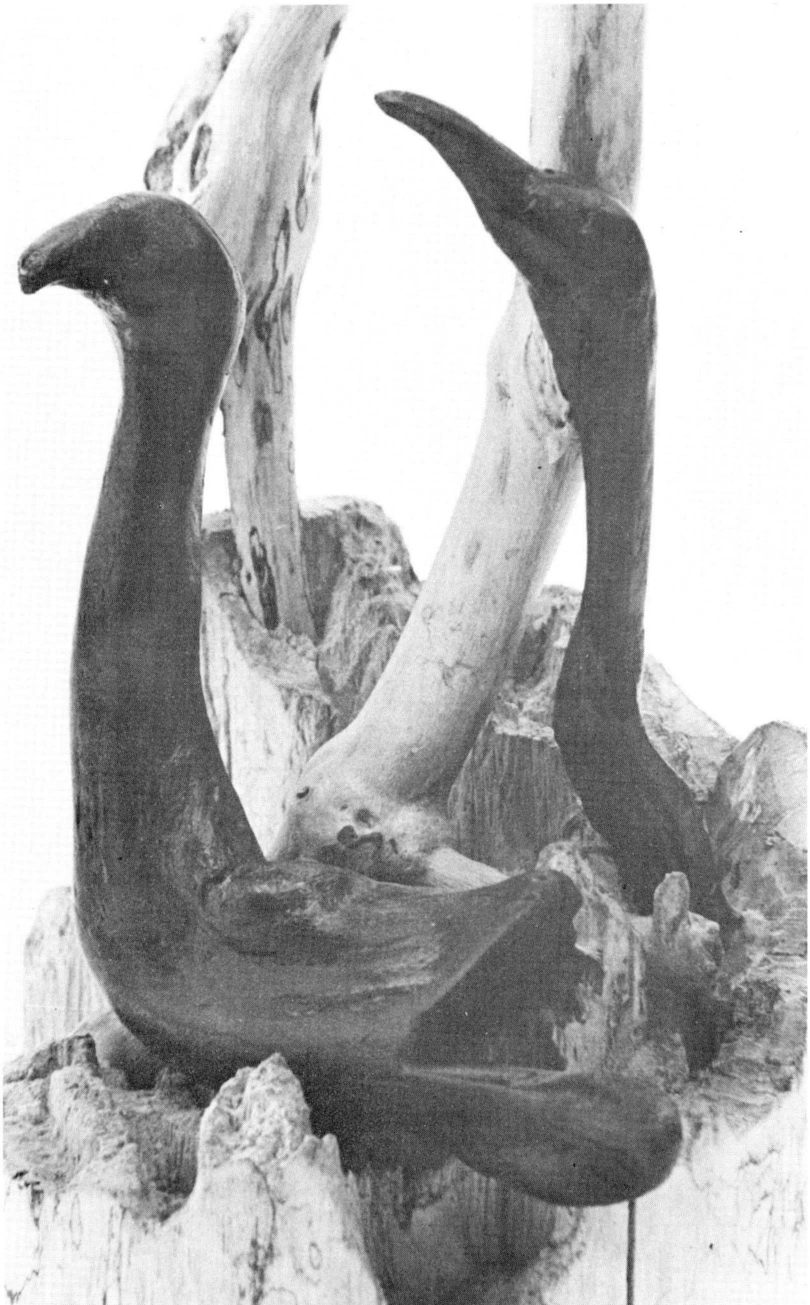

22 It was not particularly momentous to find two bird-like pieces and then, because they were not in flight, to decide that they could be at a nesting site; but it was a good first answer to the question of what to make. As found, the birds had long necks and sharp beaks, suggestive of seabird divers, which nest on rocky cliffs. A section sawn from the end of a thick and splintered driftwood branch proved ideal for their sort of nest. It also provided a strong, stable base and rigid support for the 'tree' uprights. The open-minded approach paid dividends and everything fitted smoothly into place; it just had to be called 'Two Birds Nesting' (see also plate 1). Painting the birds matt black gave emphasis to the main subject, which was later used in a floral display.

5 Making a start

How do you make a start when you do not know what you are going to make? That is precisely what this chapter is all about.

If you have been extremely fortunate and found a piece of driftwood which almost immediately suggested the finished product, then set to with great enjoyment and enthusiasm and do it. But there is no need to rely on a sudden stroke of good luck like this; nor is there any reason to be the least bit concerned because you don't know what you are about to create. If you would like to convince yourself of this right now, stop reading this chapter just long enough to have a good look at the driftwood sculptures illustrated in this book. Not one of them was preconceived when the driftwood was originally picked up on the strand-line. When the work on each one was started its ultimate compostion and shape was completely unknown. This is what makes driftwood so unusual and fascinating. It may sound strange, you may not yet believe it; but by the time you have completed your first sculpture you most certainly will.

The very fact that you do not know what you are about to create can be an asset. It leaves your mind and imagination free, open and unbiased – the ideal conditions for original creative work.

Consider the problems of a sculptor in stone. He will make detailed studies on paper outlining shape and form, decide on the type of material to be used. Perhaps he will make a prototype in clay. He has many problems to solve before picking up his tools to strike the first blow.

The artist, too, has his preparatory work. It is doubtful if there was as much enjoyment for him cutting, stretching and priming his canvas as you had collecting your raw material. No need for you to visit the artist's colourman and buy expensive tubes of paint. He must decide on a subject – still-life, model, landscape, portrait or whatever.

The driftwood sculptor has none of these things to worry about. He accepts the challenge of nature, which provided the material and its hidden beauty that his art will strive to reveal.

First stages

You can start just as soon as you have found a piece of driftwood with an interesting basic shape. Begin by snipping off all small, loose or broken bits; identify the area of greatest interest and cut off any long branches which lead your eyes away from it. If there are no long branches look for balanced proportions which you can preserve and reduce the shape to a size you can comfortably handle.

Use a pointed knife to clean out little awkward corners and strip away loose pieces of bark. On straight sections this will frequently peel off in long strips if it is still supple; often this will already have been done for you by the action of the sea. Initially remove only that which comes away freely. Where it clings tightly, and in places like forks, elbows and crevices, etc., be in no hurry to remove it. These parts, with their strong texture, might just come in later to emphasize differences in the surface finishes. The wood immediately beneath a bark layer which peels easily, as opposed to being cut or scraped off, can be very smooth indeed. Make every effort to protect this silky surface during the rest of the working stages; it is a useful extra bonus which will save a lot of sandpapering when it comes to the final stage of rubbing down.

When you make a driftwood sculpture advice may come from many different quarters, but the final creation will be the sole product of your ideas and how you translate them by your efforts. Doing small, simple jobs at the beginning allows you to get to know intimately the particular piece you are working with, and to build up a feeling for it. This rapport is not something which may or may not happen, it develops as you go along. It is the result of careful scrutiny, of seeing the piece from every angle, and of constant exploration with your hands.

Apart from holding things, hands are very good at finding things out. The fingers are not only sensitive at their tips, they can also 'feel' between each other and along their length. The palms, the heel and the edge of your hands can pick up sensations for you; as you work try to be aware of these aspects of feeling. Tuning your senses more finely will create an empathy and understanding for the true nature of driftwood which will become a hallmark of your work.

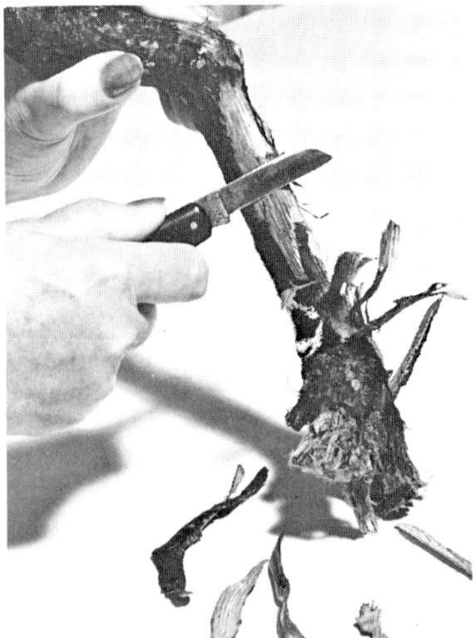

23 When driftwood is still wet the bark is relatively soft and supple, so if it needs to be removed this is a good time to do it. A pocketknife is usually quite adequate for most work; it is often no more difficult than peeling an apple. Using the knife to slice, peel and scrape will help you to clean up the wood as you go. Working with the direction of the grain will give a better finish – this is the direction which peels most easily. If the bark is too thick for a knife, prise it off with a lever.

Seeking a resemblance

Seeing and feeling are the key to what follows next, and that is to discover a resemblance within your driftwood shape to something that you already know. It does not matter how slight it is, or what form it takes. It can be quite literally anything that you know or could imagine – a human form, a head, a hand, an eye, or part of a torso. Some animal shape may have suggested itself: a horse, a dog, a bird, a lion or a fish. Maybe you thought of something from the realms of fantasy, legend or mythology, perhaps a witch, a unicorn a mermaid or some creature half man and half beast. If nothing exciting like this comes to mind then be content with something more mundane, like door knockers or dolly pegs.

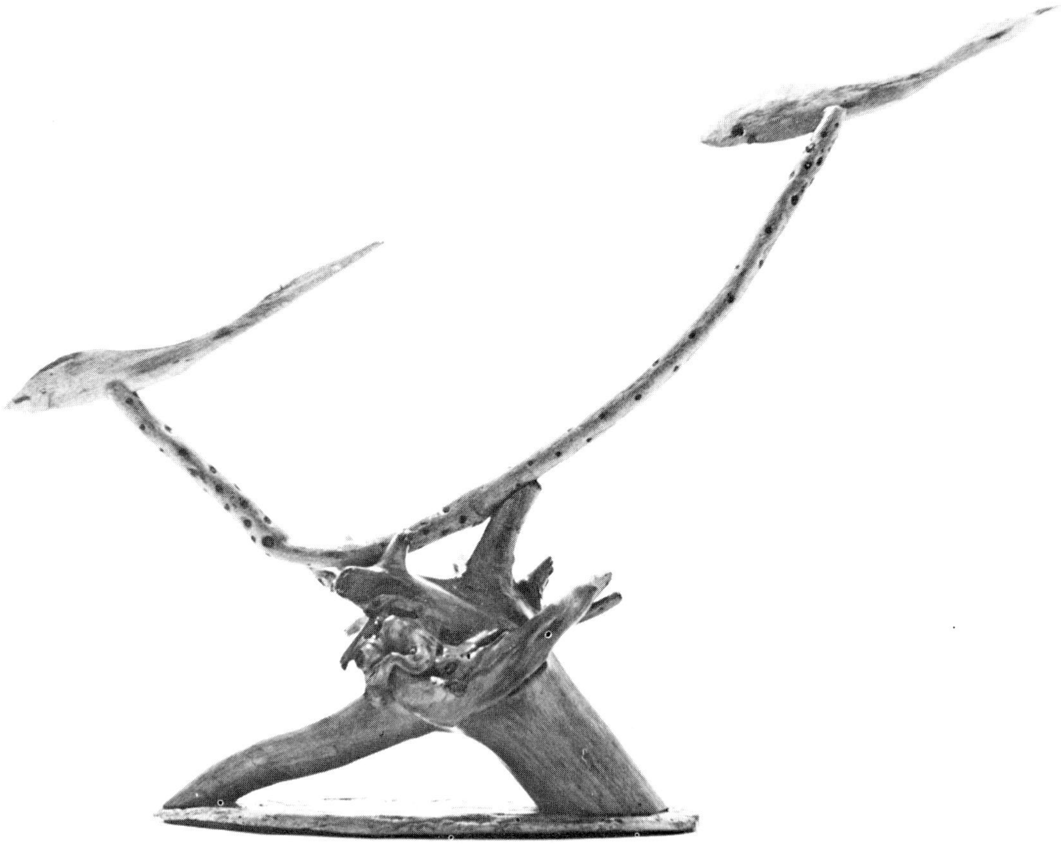

24 Here is another bird sculpture, 'Oiseaux de Mer', which provides a further example of the benefit of finding a resemblance to give you a creative starting point. The streamlined in-flight appearance of the birds when they were found has been preserved and emphasized by the slender, curved mounting. The lower portion has been curiously fashioned by the forces of nature, which also gave it the remarkably smooth finish.

At this point just what the resemblance was that you found is not all that important; later on it may change. What really does matter is the fact that you found one.

The discovery of a resemblance is a positive starting point which you can develop in a variety of ways. Look particularly at the parts which make up your new-found concept and try to define them more clearly in your mind. Do not be in too much of a hurry to start the physical defining with tools; there will be ample time for this later. Now is the time to try and get a better mental picture of the piece. Look for similar shapes; you may discover that there are several others not previously noticed. Consider whether it would be practical to cut them off and group them together in other ways. Keep your resemblance firmly in mind, and try to devise ways of emphasizing it and how it may look when it is being worked.

Exploring ideas

During the making of a driftwood sculpture there are times when you may want to change course and leave your original concept in favour of a better one. Sometimes, as you will discover, you don't have any choice in the matter; circumstances may compel you to change course whether you want to or not. The piece you are working on may break, you may accidentally make a wrong cut. Perhaps the most disturbing thing is when you get a feeling that you are being gently pushed in another direction; something you find hard to define, like a half-formed idea which does not crystallize.

If you get these intrusions into logical thought, welcome them, close your ears to the humdrum world about you and if your mind wants to indulge in flights of fancy let it soar and wander free. (Meditation of this sort is good for the creative soul!) Explore your ideas to the full but keep locked on to the driftwood in your hands, as the very feel of it will help to keep your imagination within the compass of your subject.

25 The making of Sea Eagle

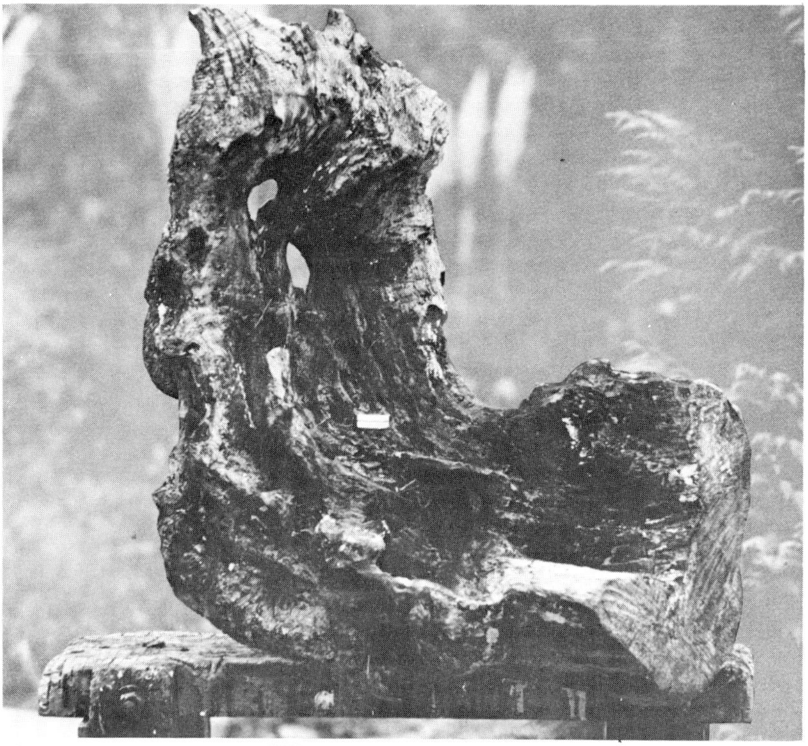

A *This piece of driftwood was too big to carry home, so it hitched a ride in the boot of the car. It had to be cut down to a size which could be more easily handled. But where to make the cut when you don't know what you are going to make? The answer lies in identifying the most interesting parts and marking them with chalk or sticky tape. This helps you to avoid cutting into them. If doubts still persist you can duck the issue and just cut it through the middle.*

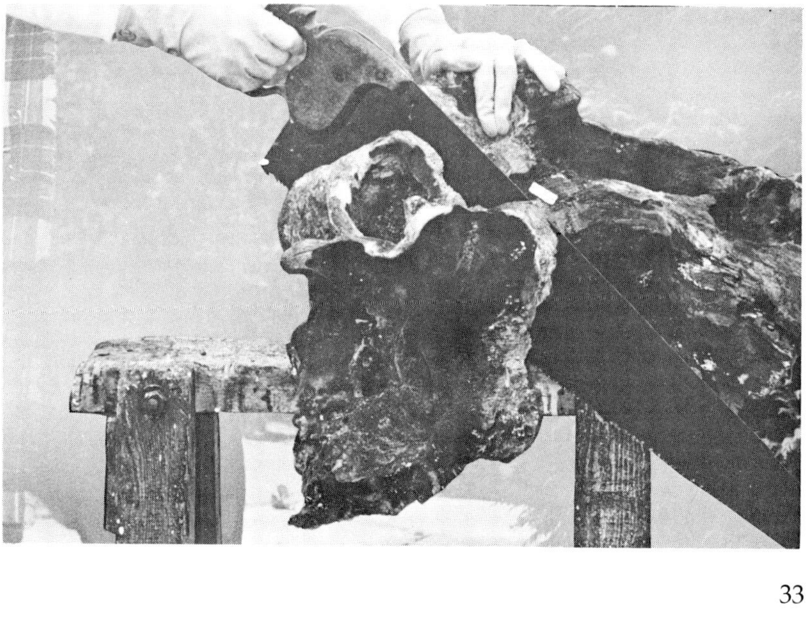

B *Sawing is not difficult if the saw is sharp and the blade is held at right-angles to the wood. Slight, steady pressure is all that is needed; use even strokes and let the teeth do the work. The small piece of white sticky tape near the top edge of the saw marks the line for cutting. Once you have started, don't try to change direction by curving the blade. If you make a clean cut it may form a good base at a later stage if the sculpture turns out to be a free-standing piece.*

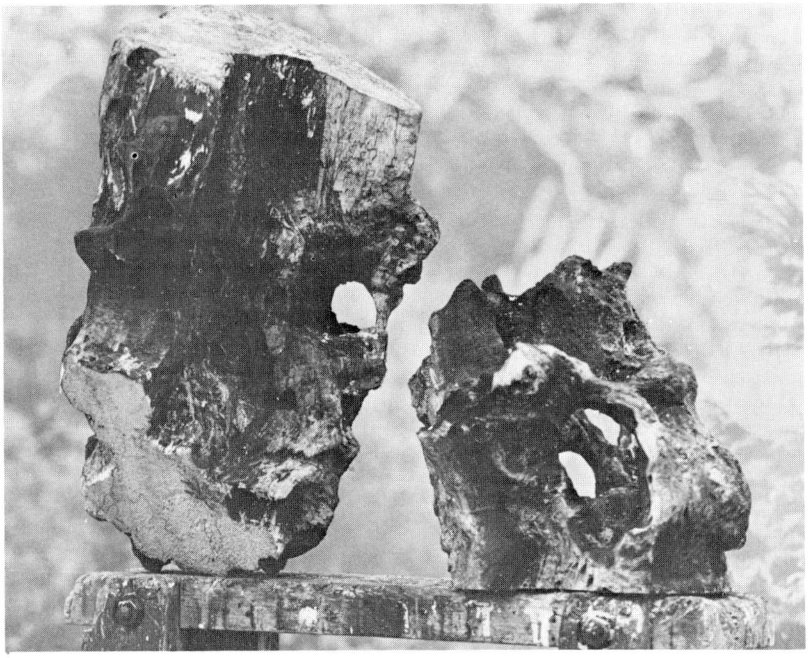

C *After sawing, the shapes seem different, so spend some time moving them around, searching for a resemblance and pondering any ideas which may arise. If nothing in particular suggests itself, the next step is simply deciding which piece to work with. It was decided to concentrate on the right-hand one. A state of uncertainty is quite natural with driftwood sculpture and is no cause for worry; instead let there be intense curiosity to find out what bit of magic lies hidden within.*

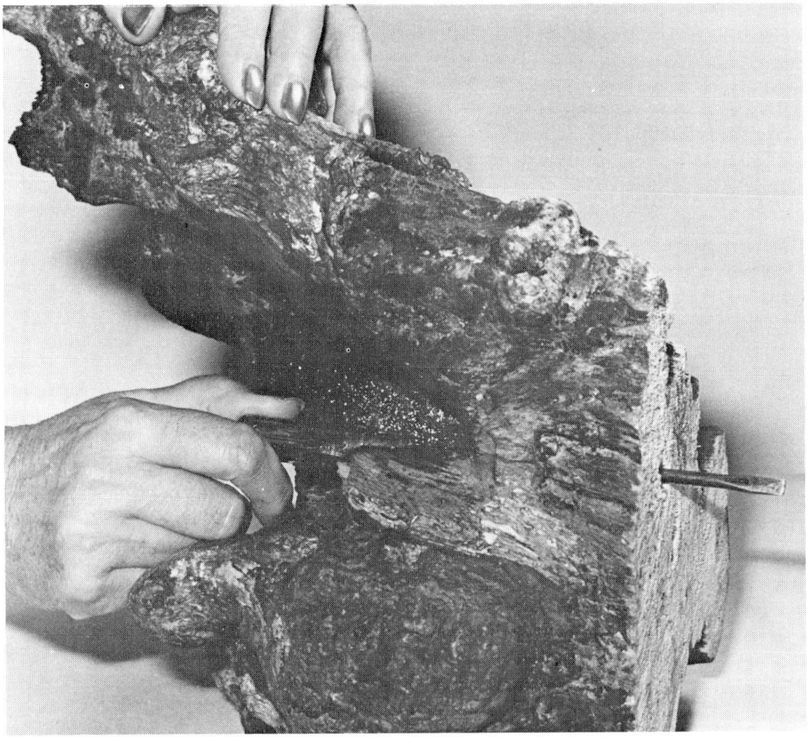

D *Part of the cut surface had a more open texture and it felt a bit crumbly. Probing with a screwdriver found a soft patch, and soft patches do not make good sculptures. There were two things one could do: either dig it out all the way back to solid wood, or do a controlled burn. The latter, being a more fascinating process, was the choice favoured.*

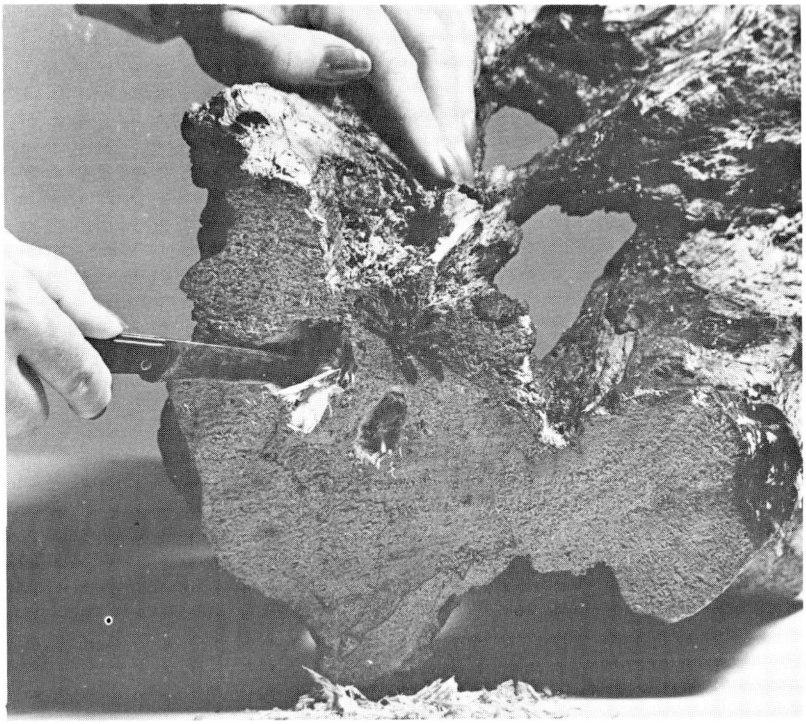

E *At the point where the screwdriver had come through, a knife was used to cut and winkle out some of the soft wood. The object was to make a hole where the fire was needed while leaving some of the loose bits in place to help the burn start more easily. The fact that there was already a little hole right the way through was an advantage because it would soon create the chimney effect.*

The fire was started with a propane blowlamp (see plate 37).

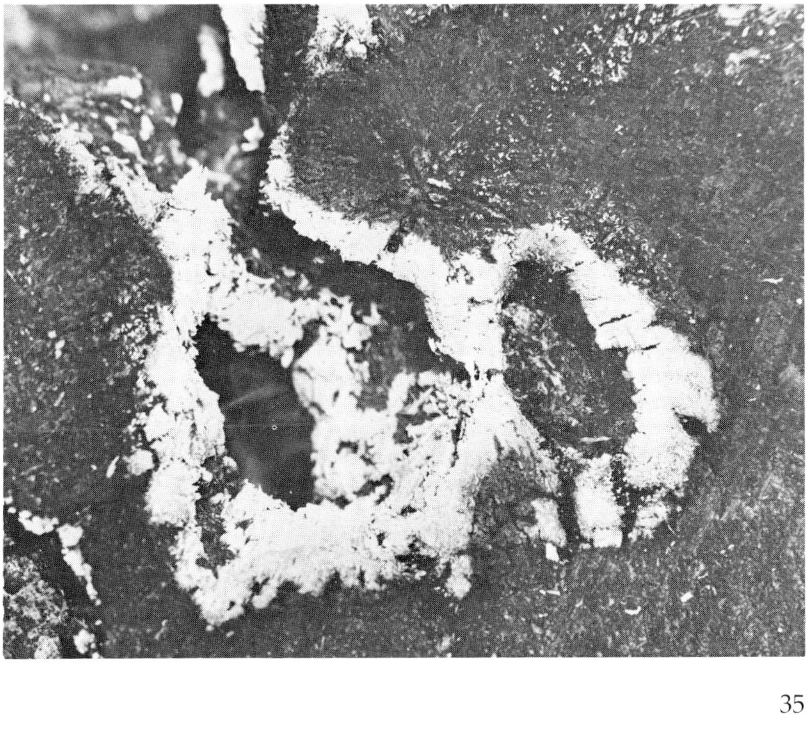

F *Soon the burning was going by itself and was beginning to form 'fire tracks' where the soft wood lay hidden. In this close-up photograph the white rings are wood ash which has formed on the surface; underneath, the charcoal glows red as the fire follows its secret paths. If there is no chimney you need to rake out a little charcoal from time to time to let the air get in to keep the burn going. Where good, sound wood which you wish to keep is being burned away it can be stopped locally by a dab or two with a small, wet paint brush. Don't lose control, and quench it all if need be.*

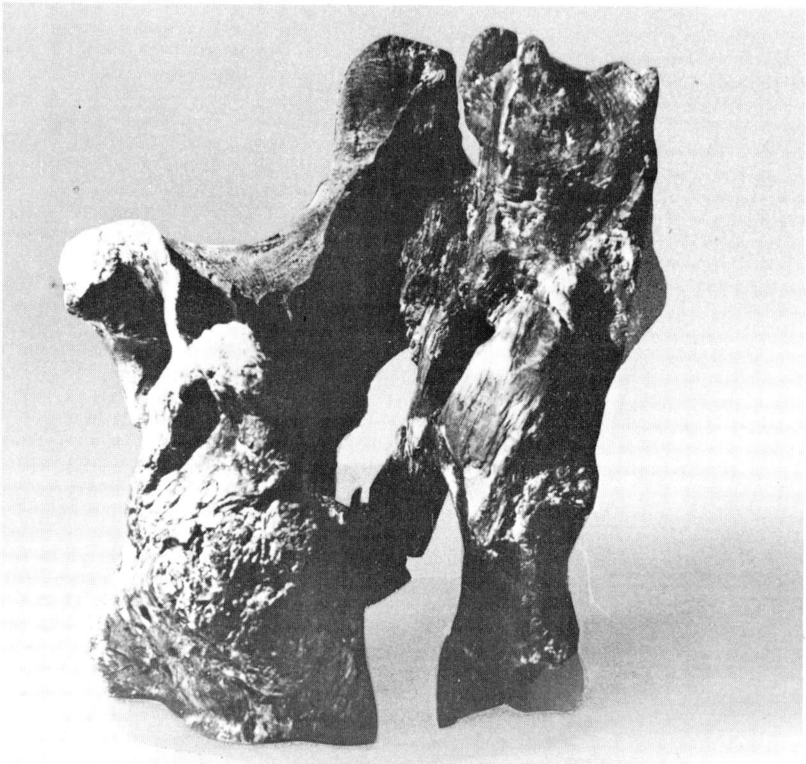

G *The fire was put out by degrees as probing with a screwdriver revealed that only hard wood was left. When all was finally quenched the piece looked like this, a charred and backened skeleton. Much of the centre core had gone and some of the original holes were now much bigger. If things look black at the moment, take heart, from here on they get better!*

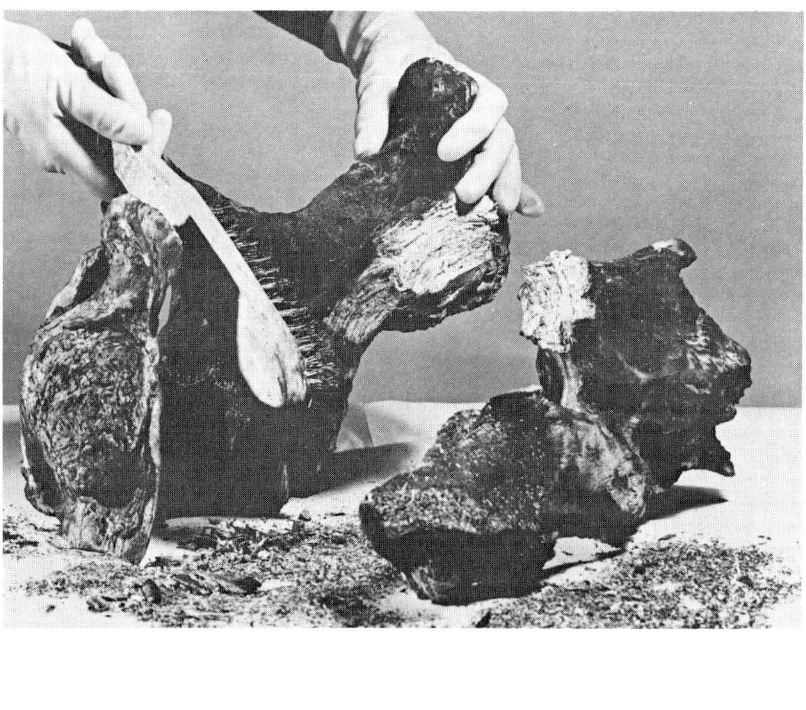

H *A wire brush shifts charcoal fast. There will be black fragments and dust floating about, so do this job outside, facing down-wind and wearing gloves. During wire-brushing the piece split in two. Perhaps this was fate taking a hand, because when the smaller piece was examined a resemblance to a bird of prey was seen. This was exciting – it pointed to a direction and a goal.*

I The break had occurred at a point where some soft wood had remained undetected, so it was taken back to the sundial in the garden where, on top of this improvised stone workbench, the burn was resumed. The resemblance to a bird of prey is beginning to emerge more clearly; it is being held by the head at an angle of about forty-five degrees and looks as if it is perching on a pinnacle or something. The knife is being used to scrape away glowing charcoal to stop this part of the wood burning away completely. This thin part later became the bird's legs. To the left of the photograph the other part, which broke away, is having its soft part burned out, though this piece will not be used yet.

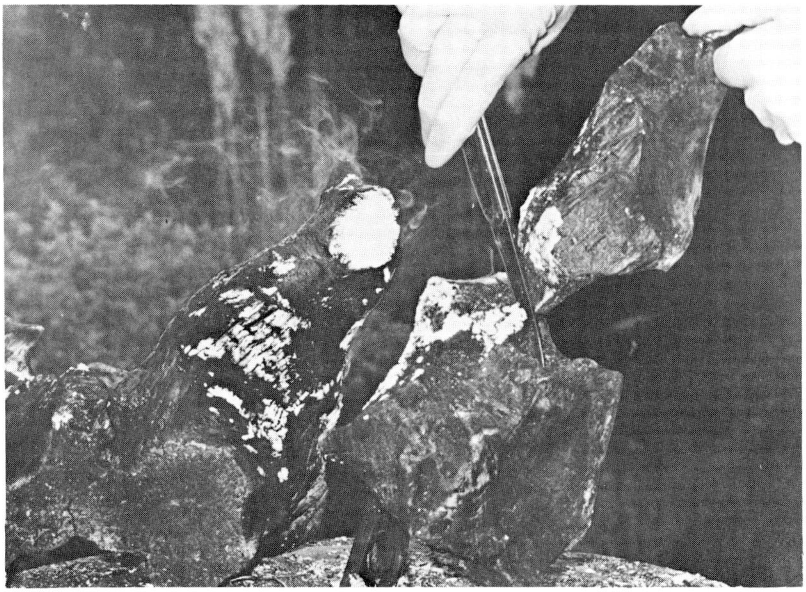

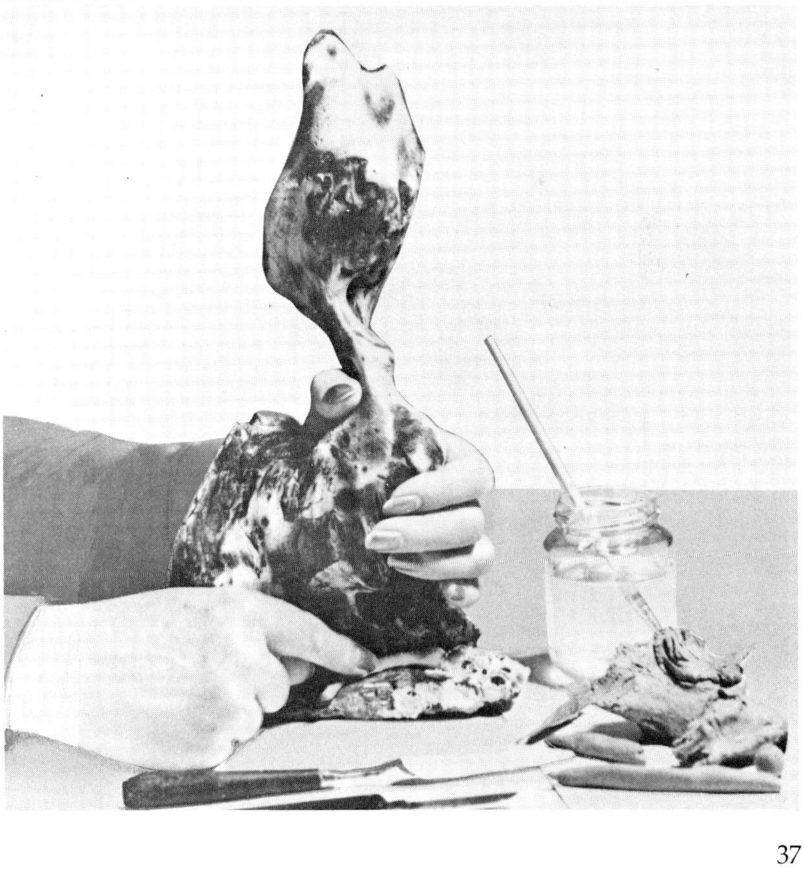

J There is now a considerable difference in appearance. The transformation was brought about simply by wire-brushing and scraping and a little shaping to the head.

In this illustration the bird of prey has already been firmly cemented with an epoxy resin to the burnacled shale base (plate 30), which was just right for size, shape and compatibility. The gaps between the driftwood and the shale are being filled with a cold-setting modelling clay. The surfaces are moistened first and then the clay textured to blend in with them. When the clay had set it was coloured with artist's acrylic paints to match both materials.

K *This sculpture has many different textures, and when its ultimate shape and form were discovered every effort was made to use them to advance the theme. The 'pinnacle' on which the bird stands was deliberately left craggy; the stone base with its barnacles add to the feeling. The legs of the bird were already smooth, and this smoothness was carried down on to the summit and then down one face of the 'crag'. The breast was originally heavily textured, and most of this was retained to indicate feathers.*

When the sculpture had been thoroughly smoothed with a fine grade of sandpaper it was given three separate coats of satin polyurethane wood-seal varnish.

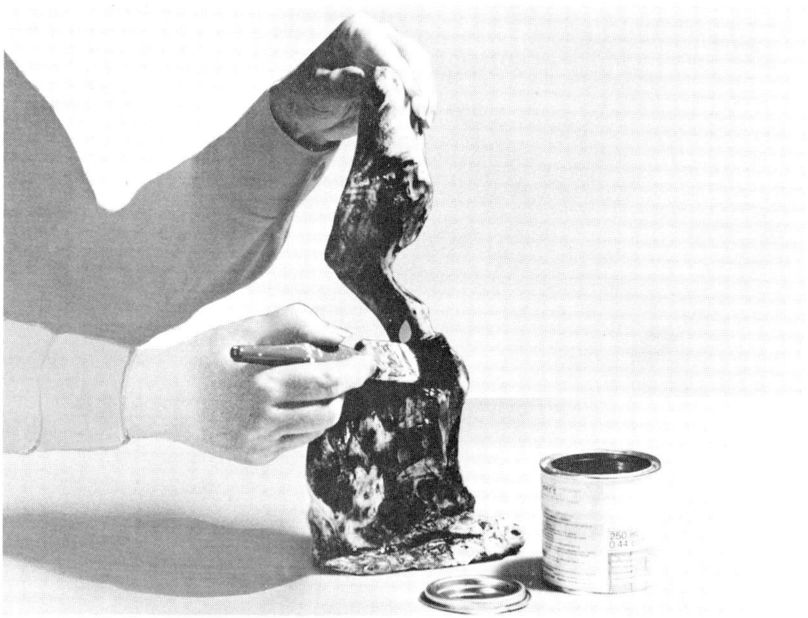

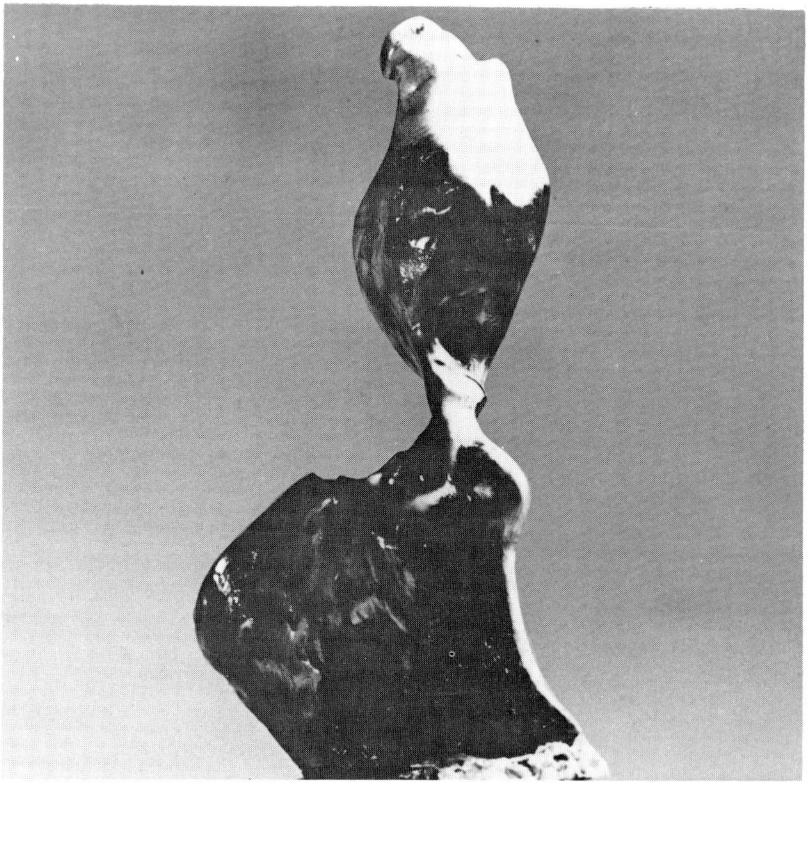

L *This is the finished sculpture. Because not only the driftwood but also the shale and its barnacles came out of the sea, this bird of prey just had to be called 'Sea Eagle'.*

Look back to the chunk of driftwood in photograph **A**. *No one knew there was a proud Sea Eagle in there just waiting to be discovered.*

6 Working stages

If you managed to get on that flight of fancy and escape into your imagination the chances are that you will now have some other useful ideas about what your sculpture is going to be like. On the other hand, if you came back to earth with a bump and still have no idea what you are going to make, do not be disheartened. It might still look like a piece of old driftwood to you, but be assured, the hidden beauty is still there and you will surely find it. All that is required is patience and some dexterity with the tools.

So far the tools have only played with the driftwood, doing simple jobs like scraping and trimming. Now is the time to get to grips with the problem and start removing some wood. With a knife or chisel probe for and remove soft surface areas; dig deeper and, should a soft patch go right through the piece, then follow it. If you make holes in the process, that's all right – go ahead and enlarge them. Be guided by what you find. If the holes are irregular and you can make them symmetrical with the surform then do this as well. The edges of holes can be squared, rounded, feathered or bevelled; consider which is most appropriate. When you uncover harder wood and different grain or colour patterns follow them carefully: as you expose them so the character of your piece will alter.

Changing shapes

Be constantly alert for a change in resemblance. As the work proceeds frequently stand back and view it from a distance, turn it round, look at it from above and below, see it in strong light and in silhouette. Close your hand and make a tiny peephole with thumb and curled forefinger and scan it slowly from top to bottom. Turning it upside-down could make all the difference – unknowingly, you may have had it the wrong way up all the time. Remember how nature created the shape that you found, and wherever possible let your own cutting follow or complement the basic forms. If you do lose your first resemblance, or if you have only got a 'door knocker' and something more interesting emerges, follow the new direction.

Adding

Ideas are elusive. Sometimes they flicker in the conscious mind and then they are gone. They can hover just out of focus – you sense they

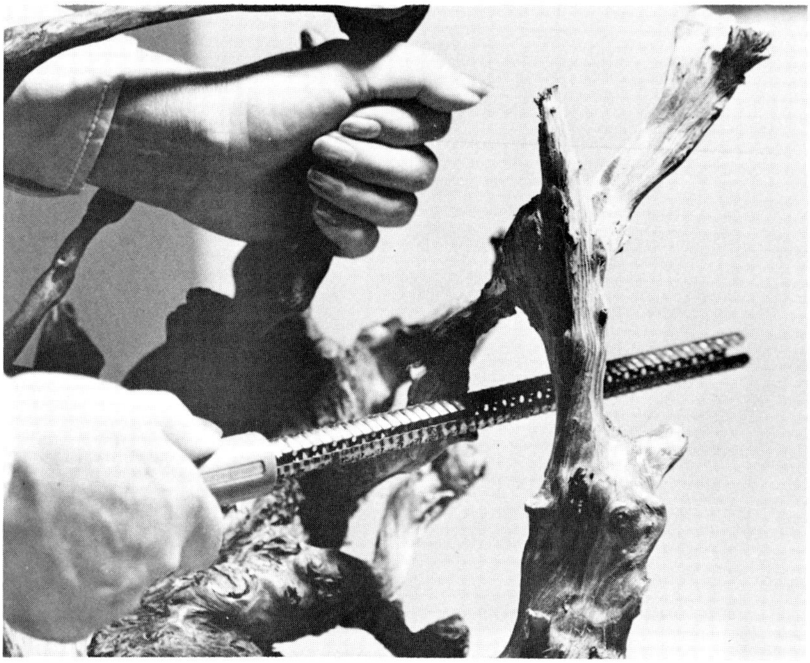

26 Rasps with flat, curved or cylindrical blades are good for removing wood and creating shapes. The kind illustrated here have distinct cutting teeth which quickly get rid of rough spikes, spurs, pimples and nodules. When shaping driftwood try to retain natural forms, and let the angles and curves that you make flow into them.

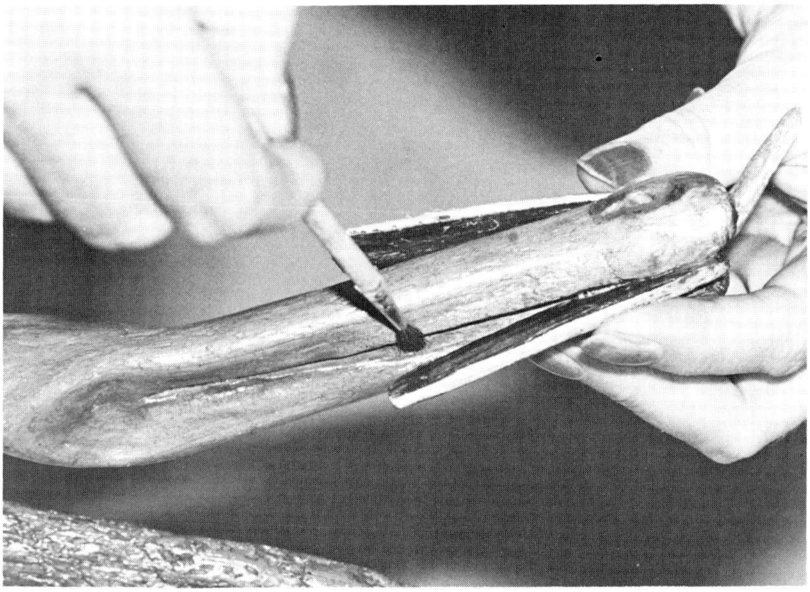

27 When nature's sledgehammers create the random shapes of driftwood some splitting of the wood is sometimes inevitable. Before casting aside such a piece consider whether the split could be used to advantage. The headdress of the 'Egyptian Storyteller' (see plate 49) was fashioned to fit into the natural split of this piece, and is shown being glued in position. Another example can be seen in 'Friend of the Seahorse' (plate 53). Here the 'Friend', the figure on the right, is cemented into and supported by a natural split in the elongated cone which forms its base.

are there but not strong enough to crystallize into the positive thoughts that will help you to create a sculpture. If this should be the case then you can help yourself to clarify them with a little more manual dexterity.

From your stockpile of raw material select a few more pieces of driftwood. Look for pieces that are not necessarily of the same type but that seem to harmonize, or contrast, with your original. Then take one piece at a time and hold it close to the original in as many different positions as you can think of and scrutinize every move you make. This is like a jigsaw puzzle: it is unlikely that you will find pieces that instantly lock into place, but you can shape them to fit in unusual ways. This method of working is discussed in the following pages, which tell the story of the birth of 'Sea Urchins at Play'.

The birth of 'Sea Urchins'

The original piece of driftwood was quite ordinary, just a length from a main branch with broken side branches. It was neither old and gnarled nor young and straight, just a happy mixture of curves and forks. Clean and well-scoured it was the sort of piece which could well have been used just as it was in a tall floral display. That was the basic idea when it was found, but too many cracks and split ends ruled against it.

So what to do with it now? The wood had a nicely bleached appearance and had a good smooth feel to it; there must be something it would make, but what? Some leisurely snipping while the problem was considered produced no answers. An ungainly section was cut away and still no flash of inspiration. A twisty bit near the bottom became a focal point which sparked briefly and then faded. The piece of driftwood was getting smaller and the pile of discarded bits much bigger before the glimmer of an idea came. When it did come it was almost like some kind of sick joke not to be taken too seriously; where a branch with a split end forked, one bit looked like a clothes peg, an old-fashioned, oversized dolly peg. A question which will forever remain unanswered is, what saved it from being chucked on the bonfire there and then?

Dolly pegs ! Not very promising, but at least it was a starting point of sorts and that was the main thing. 'Keep an open mind,' the man said. But what can you do with a bunch of dolly pegs? Polished and fastened down on a baseboard you could not even use them for hanging out the clothes! Then suddenly the next idea came. It need not be a bunch of dolly pegs and forget the clothes – it could be a group of figures. This was a much more encouraging prospect: a group of figures had far greater potential. Once you have found an objective and a direction in which the work can go, interest and enthusiasm reappear to stimulate the effort. This case was no exception, and the search was now on for some kind of 'figures'.

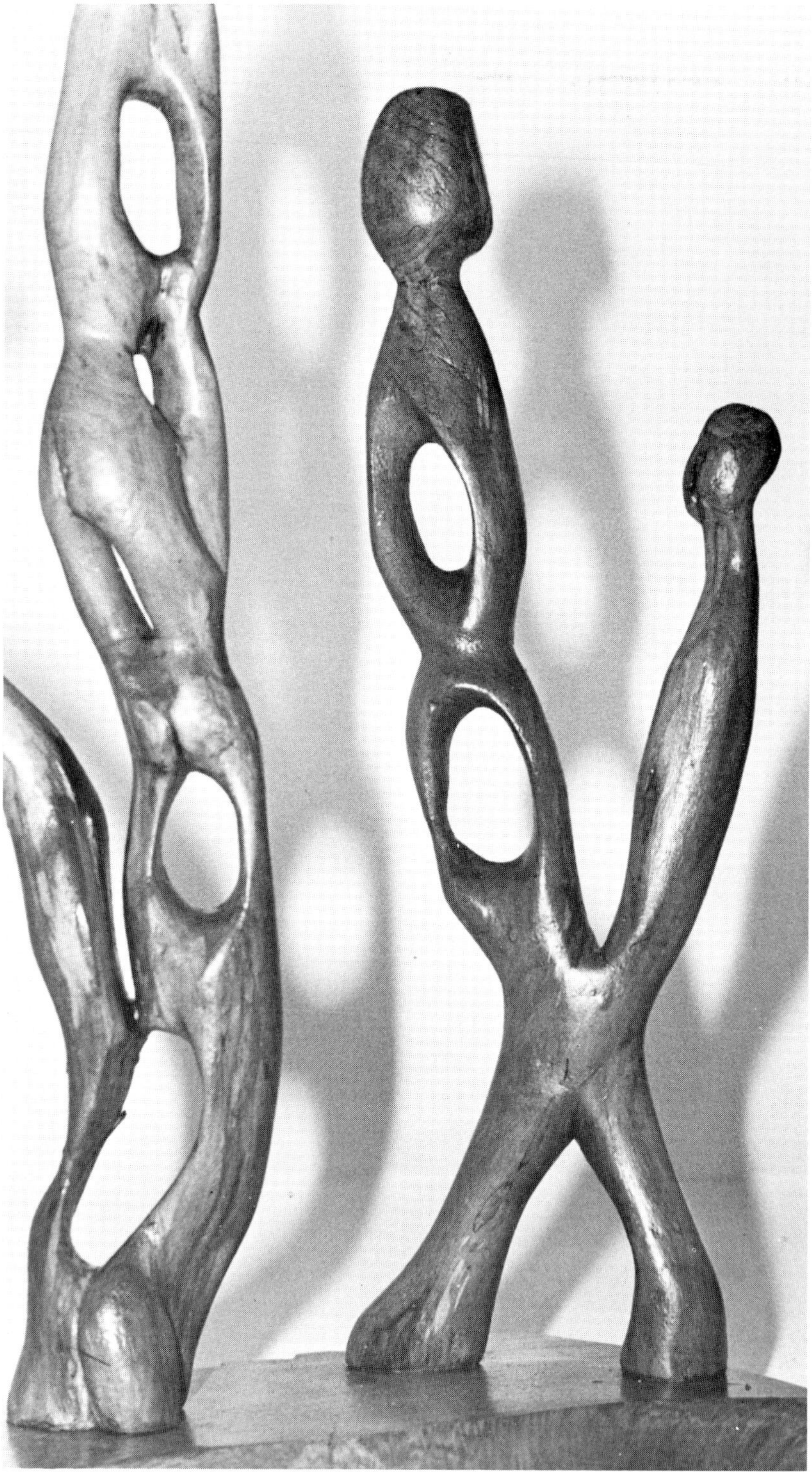

28 Part of the 'Sea Urchins' sculpture that sparked off the idea of Siamese twins. At least it was a more interesting thought than 'dolly pegs'; exploring these new possibilities eventually led to the idea of a group of figures. The body-holes were made later.

When cutting out one of the forked sections it was noticed for the first time that two parts had grown together with a Siamese twins effect and were joined at a part which could conceivably make a 'head'. Although it seemed a useful feature to try and preserve, unfortunately it split, and the one head became two. A setback, but no need to worry; after all, eminent surgeons go to great lengths to separate Siamese twins, and here were two separating themselves. It is funny the way things work out with driftwood; at the start there was nothing to go on, then it was all about dolly pegs, and when the original large piece had all been cut up the bench seemed full of figures. Figures? Well, bits with figure potential, and there was another still-intact Siamese!

Trying out ideas Perhaps it was the ideas about 'Siamese' which preordained that this 'group' was going to be abstract human. Seeing them littered about the bench one could be forgiven for thinking them more like a group of outsize stick insects. To lessen this impression the lower sections were cut to equal lengths with a small saw, and this solved the 'one leg longer than the other' problem. The 'things' were now free-standing (to call them figures at this juncture was too optimistic), and some time was spent trying to make them fulfil the 'group' concept.

The result was disappointing, and after studying various trial arrangements it became clear that some of the elements were not compatible. The only bits that seemed to fit in with the group idea were the two Siamese types, so the rest were scrapped. This meant that there were not enough members to form a quorum and a consequent job vacancy arose for two or more free-standing figures to join a group.

There followed a leisurely search through the driftwood stock, which yielded some compatible-looking pieces and, most surprising of all, there was a forked branch which looked like two Siamese figures joined at the knee. There seemed to be no escaping the fact that everything was suddenly going Siamese. When you are working with driftwood, these strange little encounters and shifts of emphasis happen too frequently to be just coincidence. Maybe you do pick up vibrations from the stuff!

So, if these little people wanted to be Siamese twins it seemed logical to try to help them, and when a length of springy vine turned up in the stock box it was decided to try to link them all together. Holes just large enough to take the vine were drilled through the figures in positions that would hold them together in a circle. They were then threaded on, the vine passing twice through each; the idea was to move them around in search of an interesting composition. Because of the springy nature of the vine as it was forced into tight coils, the whole thing almost immediately erupted into a kind of animated puppet show. It soon became obvious that only two hands could not pose five jumping figures, but the exercise did yield a good crop of new ideas.

The vine had certainly linked the units together but the effect was not right. It all seemed too artificial, so the vine was unthreaded and discarded.

The real benefit was that now, for the first time, the 'dolly pegs' had crystallized into a group of children at play. The name 'sea urchins' was to come later. After an impoverished start with no ideas, they were now coming thick and fast. They were playing tag, leapfrog and piggy-back – and for the latter two games the Siamese connections also seemed right.

Shaping the wood now became very important. Every part had to be slimmed down. The holes drilled for the vine were enlarged to the maximum to create framework body shapes. Spaces between legs were made and tapered. Heads, necks, waists and buttocks, thighs and knees – every part of the driftwood that could be defined in bodily expression was carefully sought out and fashioned.

In the centre of the group the tallest figure was made by mounting one half of the original Siamese twin on top of an unrelated, but compatible, piece of driftwood from the raw material stock box. The other part of the same Siamese can be seen at the extreme left of the group in plate 32. The only clue that they were ever joined can still be seen in the shape of the heads.

The unrelated lower part of the central figure was made to match the others by making the oval-shaped holes. The actual joint between upper and lower parts was made with pins and adhesives. The pins were simply two round nails with their heads removed and located in small pilot holes drilled into both surfaces. After a trial fitting to make sure the joint seated properly the adhesive was applied and left to set.

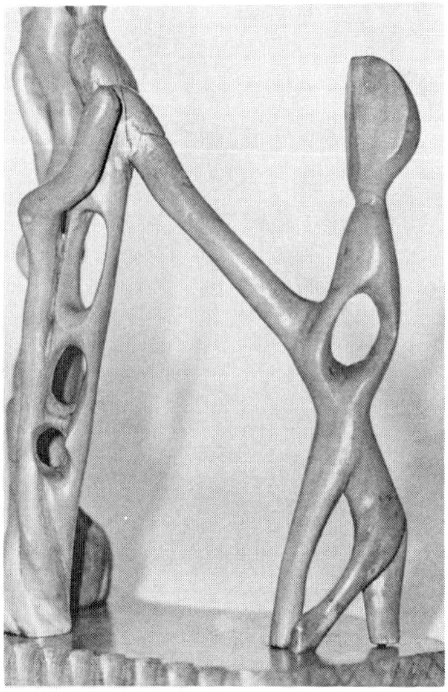

29 This figure was part of a Siamese twin until the join at the head was accidentally broken during the working. It was matched with a compatible piece and now forms part of the two left-hand figures shown in plate 32.

Finding a base board The sculpture at this point consisted of three pairs of figures. To keep them upright and preserve their action meant finding a baseboard on which they could be permanently mounted. Another hunt through the raw materials stock box produced a splendid piece of oak driftwood about 25 mm thick. At some stage in its past it had been part of a plank sawn from the outer part of the tree, because one edge still had bark on it. This peeled away easily, revealing beautiful smooth curves and an edge with a natural slope, ideal for leading the eye in and gently upwards.

The other three edges of the baseboard were square and severe, too contrasty by far in relation to the gentle flow of the front edge. This problem was resolved quite easily by using a round surform to serrate the back edge with sloping notches. The two short ends were left square but their corners were rounded. Three small nail holes in the top were filled with a plastic wood made from oak sawdust mixed with a little glue and colour-matched with a little raw umber colour.

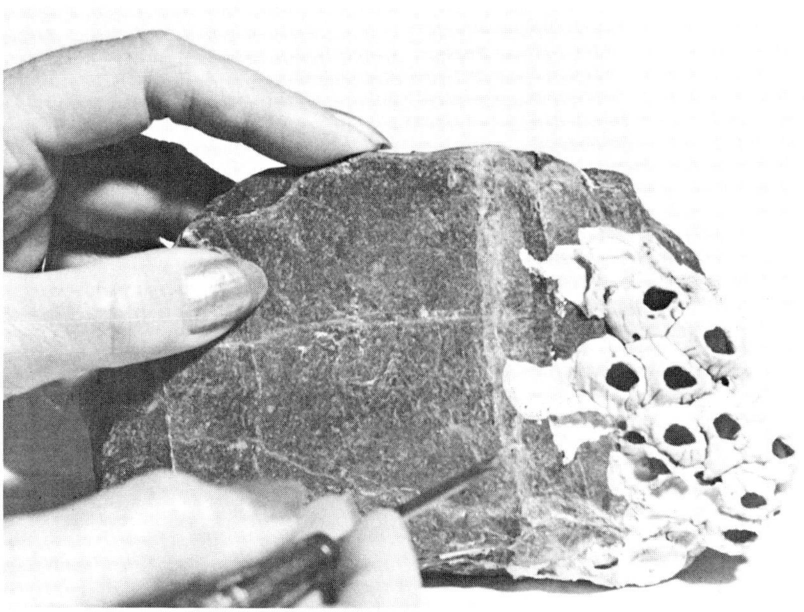

*30 Bases do not have to be of driftwood. You could use any natural object which complements and adds interest to your sculpture provided that it can be securely fastened and gives good stability. This piece of shale has been colonized by barnacles; conveniently, they only lived at one end, leaving the rest free for a driftwood sculpture. Broken and untidy bits were chipped off with a screwdriver and sharp edges rounded with a file. Later, this piece made a base for 'Sea Eagle' (see plate 25***L***).*

The whole board was then sandpapered smooth. Although the underside does not show it was treated in the same way for the simple reason that it provides a good surface on which to stick a soft baize or felt. (A material like this is recommended for all your sculptures; apart from the obvious benefit in protecting other surfaces on which they may stand, it does give your work a more professional finish.)

When collecting driftwood keep a keen eye open for pieces which will make bases and mountings. They do not have to be flat and smooth like this one, as a glance at some of the other illustrations will show. They will always come in handy.

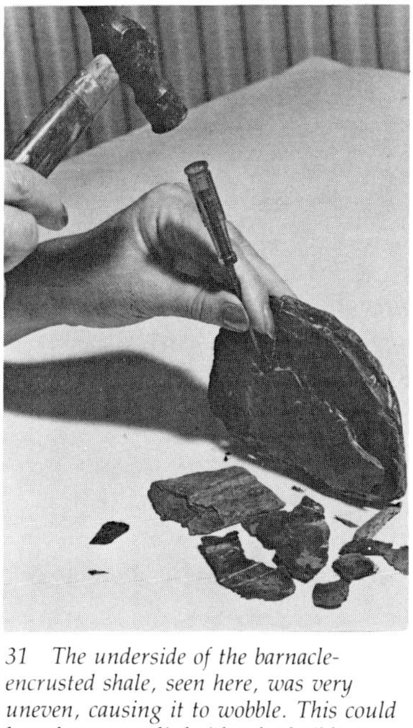

31 The underside of the barnacle-encrusted shale, seen here, was very uneven, causing it to wobble. This could have been remedied either by building up the level with cold-setting modelling clay or by chipping away the ridges. Being shale, which splits easily, like slate, the latter technique was chosen. All that was needed was gentle tapping with a hammer and screwdriver, working in the direction of its natural strata.

Trial assembly Many ideas had germinated along the way, and by constantly exploring the best ones good progress had been made. From random pieces of somewhat indifferent material there had finally emerged the basic shapes of children playing. At the moment they were still a bit ragged, like street urchins, but that could be put right. Wait a minute, they were not street urchins – being made from driftwood they must be sea urchins. Suddenly the name had clicked into place, it just had to be 'Sea Urchins at Play'. It seemed to be exactly right, and all the other names which had constantly been flickering in the mind could now be forgotten.

Now, for the first time, the mental jigsaw puzzle which had started

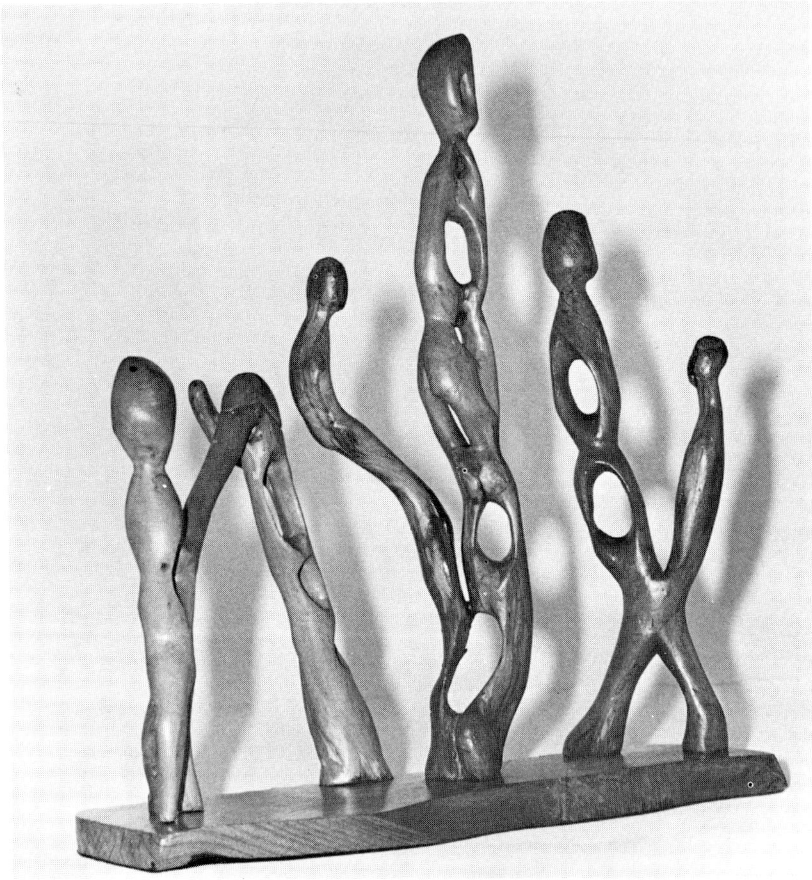

32 Here is the completed 'Sea Urchins', now alive with movement. The upper part of the tallest figure was originally the half-twin, joined by the head, of the one in plate 29.

way back on the tide-line was solved. It was a moment to be savoured, almost as rewarding as the final touch when a sculpture is finished. All effort was now concentrated on refining the shapes. Pencil and chalk were used to mark the parts where further wood could be carved away. Children are slim and agile creatures, full of life and movement, so the chunky appearance of some of the parts had to be slimmed down. There was also the need to make the individual pieces relate to each other. Above all it was important to create a natural flow of movement by emphasizing the graceful curves and streamlining the holes, so that the eye has an easy and uninterrupted traverse around the group.

After the cutting tools had been finally laid aside, rasp, file and sandpaper in ever finer grades were used to achieve a silk-smooth surface. After buffing with a soft cloth, various trial assemblies were made to find the most effective compostion.

The final fixing Having decided on the final arrangement of the figures, their positions were marked on the baseboard by drawing

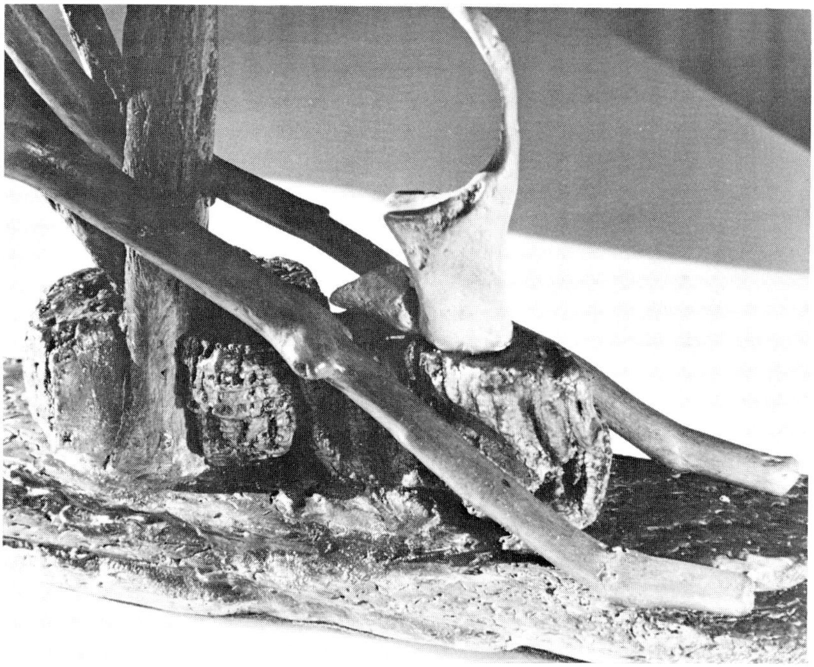

33 During trial and final assembly it is important to consider the stability of your sculpture on its intended base. At least some major parts should fit closely together and be capable of being screwed and glued to each other. Additional stability also comes from component parts giving rigidity to one another; in the 'Egyptian Storyteller' the base has seven fixing points (see also plate 49).

lightly round the bottom of each one with a pencil. In the centre of each a hole was drilled down through the top surface, slightly larger than the diameter of the brass screws. On the underside the holes were then counter-sunk to permit the screw heads to lie flush. Small pilot holes were made in the bottom of each figure to help the screws to start and to limit the risk of splitting the wood.

After a final check to make sure all was in order, a bead of strong adhesive was placed under each foot and the screws put in and tightened; then the whole was laid aside to set. Later the underside of the baseboard was covered with a piece of green felt. This was first cut to shape and then fixed with a waterproof adhesive. This sculpture was smooth and close-grained, and for this reason it was decided to give it a wax finish (on rough-textured surfaces wax will clog and is not to be recommended). Then, after plenty of buffing to get a good natural shine, it was 'Sea Urchins at Play' for ever.

7 The creation of 'Nautilus'

It may sound odd to describe one driftwood sculpture as being different from others when no two are ever alike. But there are usually some common factors, if only in things like being made from wood which is old, weathered and gnarled and being in the sea a long time. But 'Nautilus' really was different. It came from very young stock, a mere sapling in fact. Its end as a tree must have been swift; torn from mother earth, it died with its roots on. This must have been the hand of fate because it was from the root section that 'Nautilus' eventually emerged as a sculpture.

At the time it was found as driftwood it had no name and no identity, which is true of all driftwood sculptures, but then there was another difference – the condition of the sapling. Every last shred of bark had gone, and every vestige of earth, sand and clay had been washed away. It was so smooth, and as clean as a whistle. This tree had certainly seen some turbulent water in its young life and yet it had the resilience to survive in one piece and in this pristine condition.

Why it became 'Nautilus' and was fashioned in the way it was will never really be known; driftwood sculptures seem to control their own destiny. In retrospect its making is now seen as a catalogue of human error. The way of it is told here to illustrate how you can lose your way, be plagued with nebulous ideas and blind gropings which at times appear pathetic and futile, and yet these things always seem to resolve and mature into a worthwhile sculpture. It is these forays into free thinking and their surprising results which make this art form so different, and so satisfying when another unique sculpture is created.

Saplings are not usually taken for driftwood sculpture as they tend to lack character. This one was as tall as a horse and too big to store. The straight, slender trunk seemed to be the best part, so it was sawn off just above the root; a spot decision, and one which was immediately regretted. It is often good policy to cut well above this point – even if the extra length was never used it would make a 'handle'. So be it, the die was cast and there was no going back.

The slender trunk was examined, and although the wood was beautiful and firm it was devoid of any interesting or unusual features. Just a great dearth of ideas, not even a ripple; there were certainly no vibrations coming from this bit. This called into question the reason for collecting it in the first place; perhaps it was because it was free and there was not much about on that particular day. A resolve was made to be more selective in future, as there would otherwise always be a storage problem.

The shape of space

Interest in this piece was initially at a low ebb because ideas had not yet started to flow, almost to the point of reaching for an easier and more inspiring piece to work with, when something prompted a closer look at the discarded root section. This was twisted and intertwined, as roots usually are, and pathetically thin and spindly; it was not so much the roots themselves as the shapes of the spaces between them that caught the eye. This in itself was different: eyes are usually attracted by solid objects, not spaces.

At this point it should be stressed that whatever inclinations, urges or irrational thoughts one may have regarding driftwood, the logical thing to do (though it seems illogical) is to follow the impulse that sparked it off. So without further hesitation a 'space probe' was started.

It soon became evident that looking for the shapes of spaces could get a bit confusing; the problem was that you could not see the space

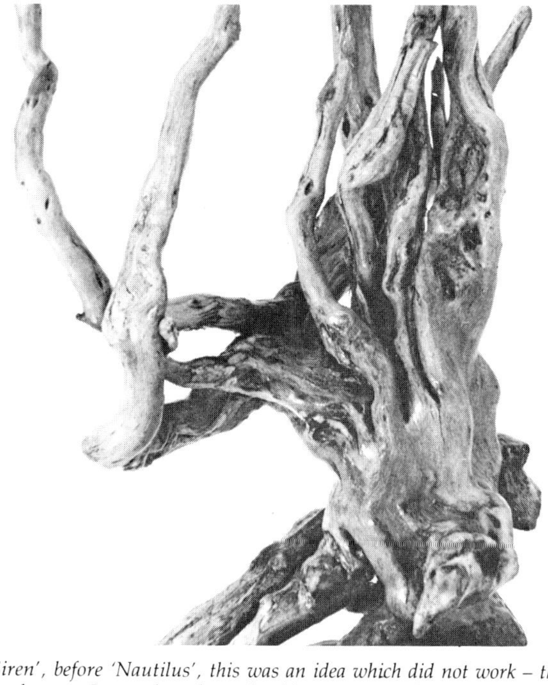

34 Before 'Siren', before 'Nautilus', this was an idea which did not work – the pursuit of a curiously shaped space. It may have been clutching at straws, but the attempt was made as part of the search for a starting point. There was not much magic around to begin with; in fact for a while it looked as though a miracle would be needed to get this sculpture going in any direction at all. Then suddenly something clicked and a mythical beast called 'Siren' popped into the picture. This idea led to others that worked, though not in the way intended.

without the solid bits surrounding it, because they made the space the shape it was. More illogical and perplexing was how to make a driftwood sculpture of an interesting isoloated intangible space. It sounded more like a job for the Invisible Man. Be that as it may, at least something had attracted the attention, and provided a starting point which could be explored.

In order to define the shapes of the spaces more easily a pair of secateurs was used to snip away the many small, insignificant rootlets that obscured them. This considerably reduced the overall size of the root cluster, which now tapered from the thickness of a wrist to that of a finger.

Too much eagerness to pursue the starting point resulted in the snipping process being carried a stage too far, and it suddenly became apparent that some of the shapes had disappeared completely. (Just how you manage to lose a hole, especially a pretty one, is purely academic, and as this is a practical book the subject is deferred.) Losing these intangible shapes was quite a setback, because a concept which had been crystallizing in the mind was on the point of emerging and whatever it may have been, was also lost with them.

A new approach

The whole project was now back at square one – well, not quite, because with driftwood sculpture there is no going back. It is not like knitting, which you can just pull out and start again. This looked like a piece that did not want to be created because of the sculptor's lack of empathy. From being as big as a horse the sapling was down to a small root section and a big pile of snippings. This posed another fundamental question: what happens next?

There is something very compelling about driftwood; it does not let you give in. The answer was to forget all previous ideas and to start looking for new ones. Fortunately, with driftwood they are never far away, and another critical look at the remaining root section soon provoked other trains of thought which could be explored.

It was decided to make an approach from a new angle, to take the remaining piece of root and temporarily mount it on some sort of base. It was felt that this would bring it down to earth and give it a more positive form. A rummage through the 'bits and pieces' box produced a choice of several flat driftwood shapes for this purpose. Then a piece of cork was found which looked much better – in fact it seemed exactly right. Both size and shape were suitable and the colours compatible, and although the texture was very different the two pieces did complement each other.

With the root section's flat end (where it had been cut from the trunk) free-standing on the cork there was a marked shift of emphasis. Some of the longer roots now appeared as uplifted arms suggesting that they were beckoning, reaching out and appealing for something. Quite unexpectedly, another piece of this fascinating sculptural jigsaw dropped into place.

Mythical beasts

For some time now the need to find a name had been quietly haunting the mind and then, in a flash, this need was answered. Those uplifted arms belonged to one of the Sirens, the half-woman, half-bird creatures of Greek mythology whose sweet singing and enchanting music lured unwary seafarers to their fatal embrace. So that was it, this sculpture was going to be called 'Siren'. (You will see what happened to 'Nautilus' presently.) All this was most encouraging. Not only had a more positive starting point been found but also the ultimate objective as well.

One of the most exciting and challenging phases of making driftwood sculptures comes at this stage, when having started with only a random piece of driftwood and without any preconceived design, all your ideas come together and for the first time you have a clear concept of the sculputure you are going to make. The next point to consider was how best to make an abstract shape convey the impression of a Siren, who after all was a mythical beast.

Just what a Siren looked like is open to question; some research showed that even the Ancients could not agree on the shape and form she took. This was comforting to know because it meant that the subject had obvious latitude for artist's licence. (With some mythical beasts you need to be quite precise: a unicorn, for example, just has to be horse-like with a single horn on its forehead.)

So the work progressed: carving, smoothing, refining the shapes and striving for the 'waving-arm' concept and being alert for places to carve 'head' likenesses. It should be noted that there are occasions when other pieces of driftwood need to be added. These should, of course, be compatible, and need to be cut and shaped to fit into the overall scheme. This sculpture needed such treatment.

It was at a later stage, when everything was going well, that the unexpected happened. An extra 'arm' had been shaped and 'Siren' was undergoing a trial assembly to see how the pieces were fitting together. In this process the unit was turned upside down to view it from another angle; the uplifted, beseeching arms that had prompted the name 'Siren' were now reversed and resembled tentacles hanging down.

Another new approach – upside down

Suddenly, and for the second time, all was confusion. The thoughts of tentacles conjured up ideas of octopus and squid, as you would expect. These thoughts were persistent and would not be brushed aside; they got stronger and stronger until one thing became very clear: the sculpture just had to be made in this reversed position.

Whether the thing was upside down all along is debatable, but one thing was sure – the name 'Siren' could not now be used and another one would have to be found.

The reasons for having to change course like this are unknown, and it appears that there are some things concerning driftwood that sculptors should not pry into too deeply. One thing, however, is certain: when you get strong signals like this you don't argue, you just do it; experience will assure you that it will all come right in the end. If this was more of the magic, it looked funny magic at this stage.

As one door closes, another opens, and now it was time for reflection and a long, hard look at those dangling tentacles. It was vital to discover what new form this sculpture was going to take. After being in a good progressive stage it had reverted and was once again a nameless 'thing'. There was something fundamentally wrong, but what was it?

Working with driftwood calls for flexible attitudes, which is not really difficult because the material offers so much scope for change. This was a major setback, but there was one important point that should be remembered: a lot of work had been done on this piece and the sculptor's hands and eyes were very familiar with it. Although it was proving difficult and wayward, a strong affinity had developed which precluded any thoughts of abandoning the project.

In a more sombre mood work was resumed. Cutting, scraping, sanding, occasionally adding an odd piece to study the effect, caressing the wood with thoughtful hands and eyes and pondering the while on these strange shapes wrought by nature. Presently patience brought its own reward, and in the quiet and stillness of the mood new ideas came softly creeping in.

With the 'Octopus' thought still persisting, a small, far-away voice seemed to whisper: 'They have big eyes'. Of course! That is what was wrong. This nameless 'thing' did not have any eyes – and no head either, for that matter. The fact that an octopus does not have a separate head and that their eyes are on the side of the body anyway was of no great importance. It was not going to be an octopus after all. If it eventually turned out to be another mythical beast, it looked like being a happy one!

Once again a new direction had been discovered which opened up more interesting possibilities. A search was made to find a compatible shape which could be fashioned to fit on top of the 'tentacles' and which would be symbolic of heads, eyes or whatever. In the 'bits and pieces' box was an old, water-worn segment of a branch about the diameter of a tennis ball, all knobbly and rough in the middle but still with firm bark on the outside. This was hollowed out, scraped, filed smooth and cut to fit snugly on top of the 'body'.

Coming to life

It is surprising how the addition of only a single piece of driftwood can bring about a dramatic change. With the head in position the sculpture took on a completely different aspect. It was now coming right just as quickly as it had gone wrong in the earlier stages. At last there was encouraging progress, it was coming together as a unified piece and not just a mess of fragments searching for a home.

To make the most of this rapid change of emphasis it was decided to proceed with the mounting and securing of the driftwood on to its cork

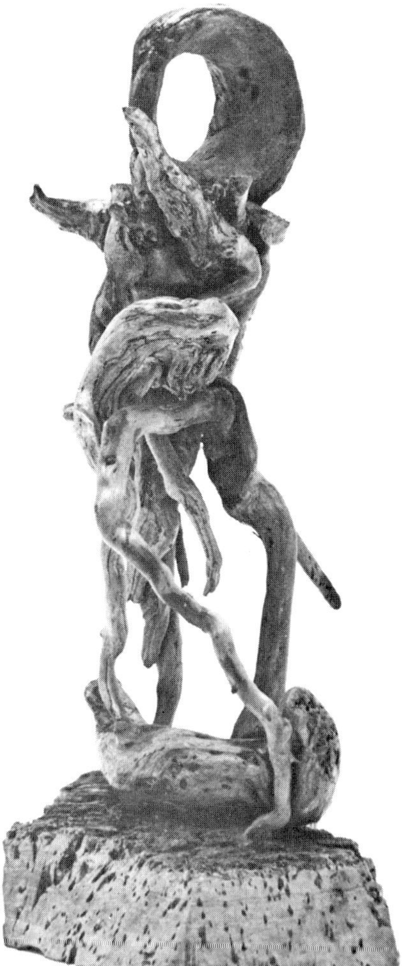

35 'Nautilus' was trouble from the word go, not because of any technical or involved working, but simply because it did not know what it wanted to be; which is an easy way of saying that the sculptor did not know. Slim and agile, like a boy full of mischief, it led the author a merry dance. Finally captured, the shape is still alive with movement and almost ready to spring into another series of frivolous capers.

base before it had the chance to escape again. The mounting process was simply a matter of drilling holes of the right size into the cork base to take the tips of the 'tentacles'. At a later stage they would be secured permanently into these holes with an appropriate glue. This was no longer a random piece of driftwood. The figure was emerging with a forceful, energetic appearance and taking on a very positive stance.

A need which quickly became apparent was to strengthen the base of the tentacles, only three of which were now in the cork – the others, being shorter, would not quite reach. Some additional piece of driftwood had to be found to link these lower appendages together to give stability and at the same time to help unify the design. The piece chosen was, when seen by itself, quite insignificant, the sort of small piece which could be picked up on almost any beach and then discarded without a second glance. For this particular job it was almost perfect: the right shape, almost the right size, with good markings and needing very little work to make it fit.

Now, finally, all the pieces had come together and were transformed into this most unusual little fellow. He was happy and lighthearted, with outstretched arms and prancing feet, not at all like that denizen of the deep which had sparked off the idea.

The remaining work was now quite straightforward. It was only necessary to check that all the parts were a good, tight fit and to work the surface up to a good finish. After all traces of dust had been brushed and blown away the parts were cemented together with a strong waterproof adhesive and left to set. At a later stage the sculpture was matt-glazed to seal the surface and bring out its rich colours.

Finding a name

The question of a name for this piece was a persistent and troublesome thought that, like the octopus, would not go away. As things subsequently turned out it was, oddly enough, the constant thoughts about the latter which solved the problem. It was discovered that there exists in the sea a family of molluscs with distinct tentacled heads, and, furthermore, that one such species is known as Nautilus, a name derived from Greek words meaning 'head and foot'. Somehow 'Nautilus' seemed very appropriate, quite in keeping with this wayward sculpture, which had been turned head to foot and top to bottom.

8 Controlled burning

What to burn

'Nautilus', you will recall, was made from the sound, healthy roots of a young sapling. At the other end of the spectrum are the heavier, gnarled limb and root sections of much older trees, which can also be used. Such pieces of driftwood frequently consist of hard, sound wood which is hidden by surrounding softer areas where decay has become well advanced. Some specimens may have been in the water for months or even years, but the fact that there is rotting wood present should not discourage you from taking it. Decay is a slow, natural process, and because much of it will have occurred in watery conditions there is seldom any unpleasant odour. It is not at all like wood suffering from dry rot; most driftwood is well washed when you find it, and perhaps the only exception would be not to take it from water which is heavily polluted.

Although driftwood in this state may not look very attractive, inside there could well be a hard skeleton which will make an extremely fine sculpture. The problem is to get these remarkable shapes out in a usable form and not to end up with piles of useless fragments. Digging, cutting and scraping is painfully slow and laborious, needing endless care and patience to avoid undue damage to the hidden hard skeleton. A bolder and much more exciting way is to burn it out. (The sculpture 'Ancient Dreamboat' illustrated in plate 40, was made by the burning technique.)

When to burn

If you decide to have a good burn-up, success depends on the driftwood being really dry all the way through; depending on its size this could take weeks or even months. It takes a long time to dry because the softer wood holds water like a sponge and these softer, wet 'veins' will run deep within the piece. When they are thoroughly dried out they make more easily combustible tracks along which the smouldering fire can travel without being extinguished by steam. As the moisture evaporates the areas of decay become dry and porous and make fire 'tracks' which burn more easily and quickly than the harder, more dense skeleton wood which needs to be saved. It is this difference in densities and burning speeds that makes the technique possible.

The process is called a controlled burn because you have to do all the controlling to avoid finishing up with just a chunk of charcoal. First and foremost this is an outdoor job, with the driftwood standing on a hard, firm surface where it can be supported or wedged firm and kept well away from other inflammables. Choose a day when there is a gentle breeze, which will help to fan the fire and blow smoke and sparks away from you and thus make the work more pleasant. Another important consideration is to have a bucket of water handy – just in case!

How to burn

Choose the softest areas of driftwood and loosen all the surface with a knife or chisel and start it burning. A blowlamp or propane torch such as a plumber would use is ideal. If you don't have one, light a small fire among the loosened bits of soft, dry wood in the traditional way. Do not use petrol, paraffin, firelighters or any other 'instant' method; the object is to get a small, localized fire going without disturbing the surface too much at the beginning. This allows the flames to settle down, and presently the fire will burn in the manner of glowing charcoal. This is where the gentle breeze comes in handy, because when the charcoal does begin to form the breeze will keep it burning steadily without your having to do all the blowing. Fire travels more easily in an upward direction, so if need be turn the driftwood over, or turn it round the better to catch the wind.

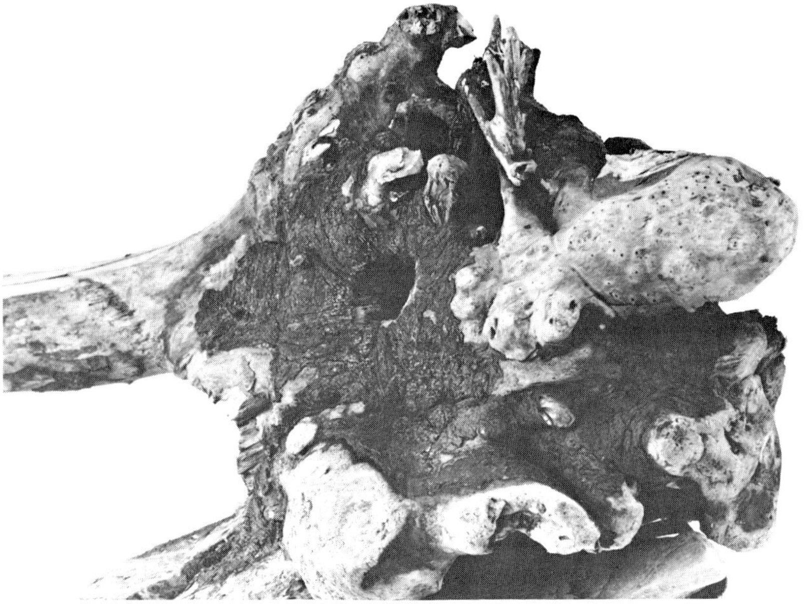

36 You could tell this hefty piece of driftwood had a lot of good timber in it by its weight, and it really felt solid when you probed and knocked on it. But there was also a lot of soft, rotted wood, much of it in inaccessible places, so it was decided to burn this away. But what on earth might it then make? Unknown to anyone, beneath this rugged exterior there lay an 'Ancient Dreamboat' and a 'Beast to Guard Treasure' (see plates 40 and 42).

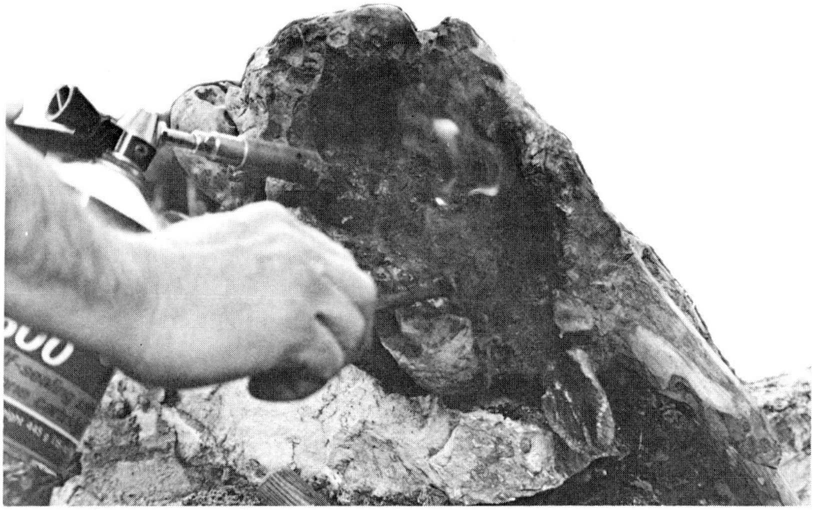

37 *The piece of driftwood was wedged into a safe and convenient position on a low garden wall and the burning started with the help of a blowlamp. Soon flames were licking gently on the surface and forming glowing embers of charcoal below. After only thirty minutes a sizeable cavity had formed in the area previously filled with dried, rotten and porous soft wood. An old screwdriver was used to scrape and extinguish the burning where hard wood was discovered.*

The glowing charcoal first burns away all the porous, decayed wood but if left it will go on to burn the harder skeleton, albeit at a slower rate, and this is where you must intervene. To prevent this happening probe and loosen the glowing charcoal in the areas which still feel soft. Where you encounter the feel of solid, hard wood beneath the crust of charcoal, scrape away the burning embers until the fire at that particular point is extinguished. It is by this process of continually probing and scraping that the fire is guided to burn away the parts which were previously rotting away.

Playing with fire

Everyone knows that you shouldn't play with fire, and yet almost everyone does at one time or another and enjoys it. In fact man has been playing with fire ever since he learned how to make and control it, and control must of course be the operative word if you are going to enjoy making sculptures this way.

As charcoal forms and burns deeper it turns white on the outside, and it is difficult to see whether or not it is still burning, particularly in strong sunlight. There may be a complete absence of smoke and the only sure way to find out is by probing and scraping off the white ash. This will stimulate the fire to glow red again before forming another coat of white as it gets deeper still.

Holes are a common feature of old driftwood and any one of them may be a fire track leading well into, or right through, the piece, and the fire should be encouraged to burn them out. Once holes do emerge in some other part of the wood they act like little chimneys, the through

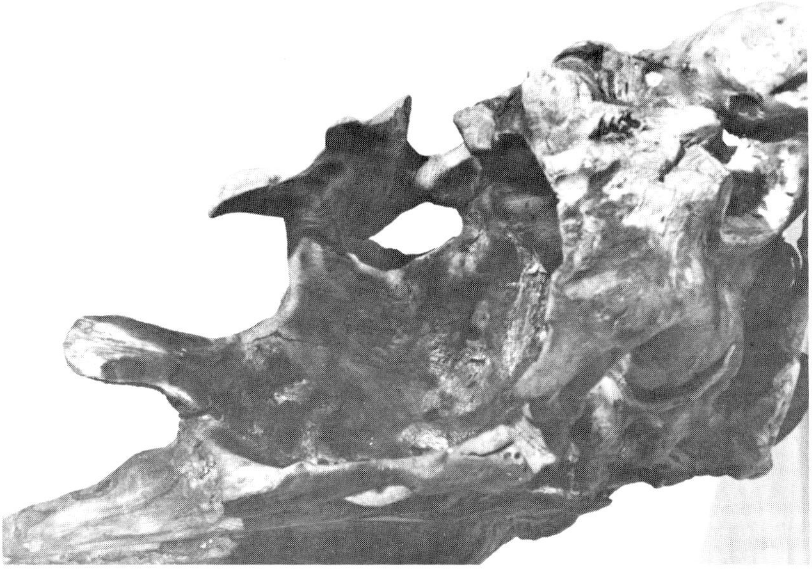

38 With the controlled burning technique you have to keep an open mind about the end result. This same piece has now changed considerably; in addition to making a large cavity amidships the fire also burned through the sides in several places. At this stage it is still just a 'something', but some idea of the final shape is beginning to emerge.

draught making the charcoal burn hotter and faster. A number of things begin to happen rather quickly. The fire may start spreading internally, which, while it is good for creating interesting shapes, may result in its getting out of control. With the increased burning rate it becomes more difficult to differentiate between hard and soft parts. Areas where the fire was scraped out to preserve the hard wood may re-ignite, or, travelling along the porous veins, the fire may burst through the surface in several places at once. The simplest way to retain control is to scrape most of the charcoal loose and tip it onto the floor to slow down the process. Only resort to the bucket of water in a real emergency because once you wet the wood it will take a long while to dry out again.

After burning

After a successful burn the driftwood may bear little resemblance to the piece you started with, thanks to the unpredictable route of the fire. The dramatic change in shape which occurs is reason enough for keeping an open mind on what the sculpture will be like, although it is possible to start forming opinions as the burning progresses. Indeed, if a clear conviction does emerge then by all means use fire-control to achieve the result; in any event you will have a very charred but interesting hard wood shape to work with.

The main job now is to get rid of all the burnt areas, which is not a

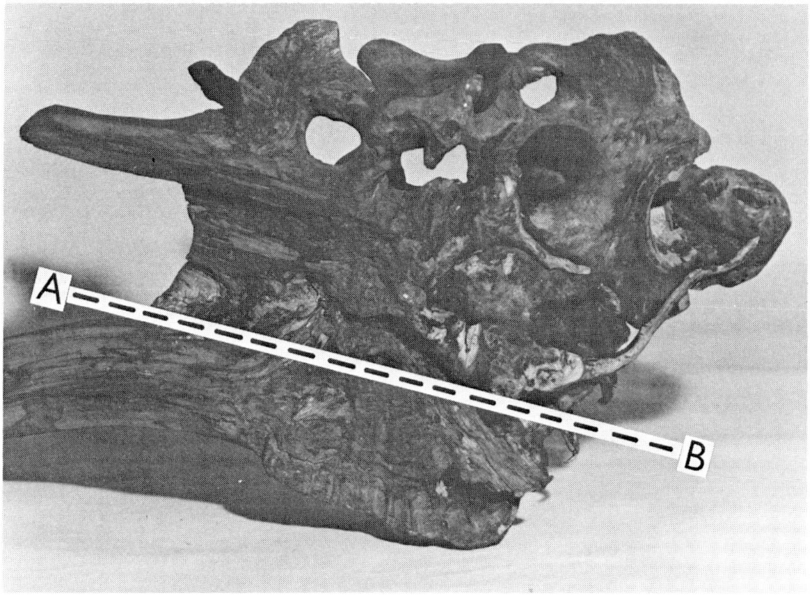

39 After patient scraping and wire-brushing most of the charred surfaces have been cleaned off. This is a time of appraisal, for finding a resemblance, emphasizing the shapes and considering possibilities. Just deciding which way up it is going to be can be a positive step forward. In this case it was the cavity which was to be uppermost. Another critical decision was to saw the piece in half at the line A—B.

difficult task. Wire-brushing and using tools with a rasping and scraping motion will remove charcoal, which comes away quite easily when cold. The charred surface beneath also scrapes away well and the wood recovers its natural colour and grain patterns, and responds well to the general finishing techniques of smoothing with wire wool and sandpapers until the surface is ready to accept glaze, polish or wax.

The 'Holy Man' (plate 41) emerged from the controlled burn of an old log section, but in the beginning nobody could have guessed he

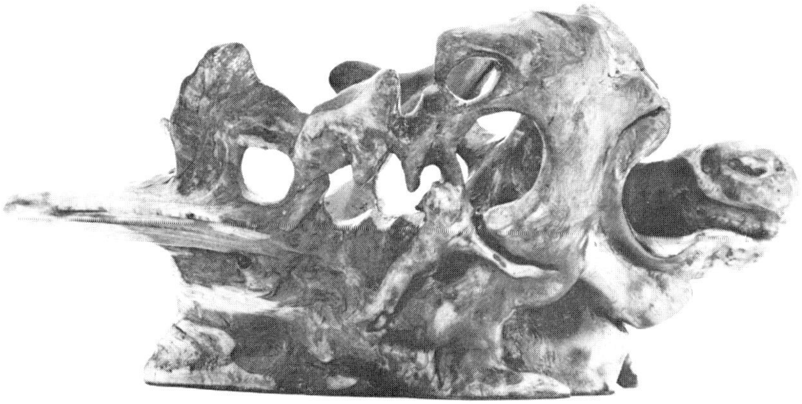

40 'Ancient Dreamboat' was the sculpture that finally emerged from the embers of the controlled burning; a far cry from the wild driftwood in plate 36. The same piece also produced a 'Beast to Guard Treasure'.

was in there. It was only after the fire had come through the surface in several places that 'eye sockets' became apparent and the idea of a mask began to form.

With the burning technique for driftwood sculpture you are never sure what will come out next; if you believe in mythical beasts a phoenix could be just around the corner.

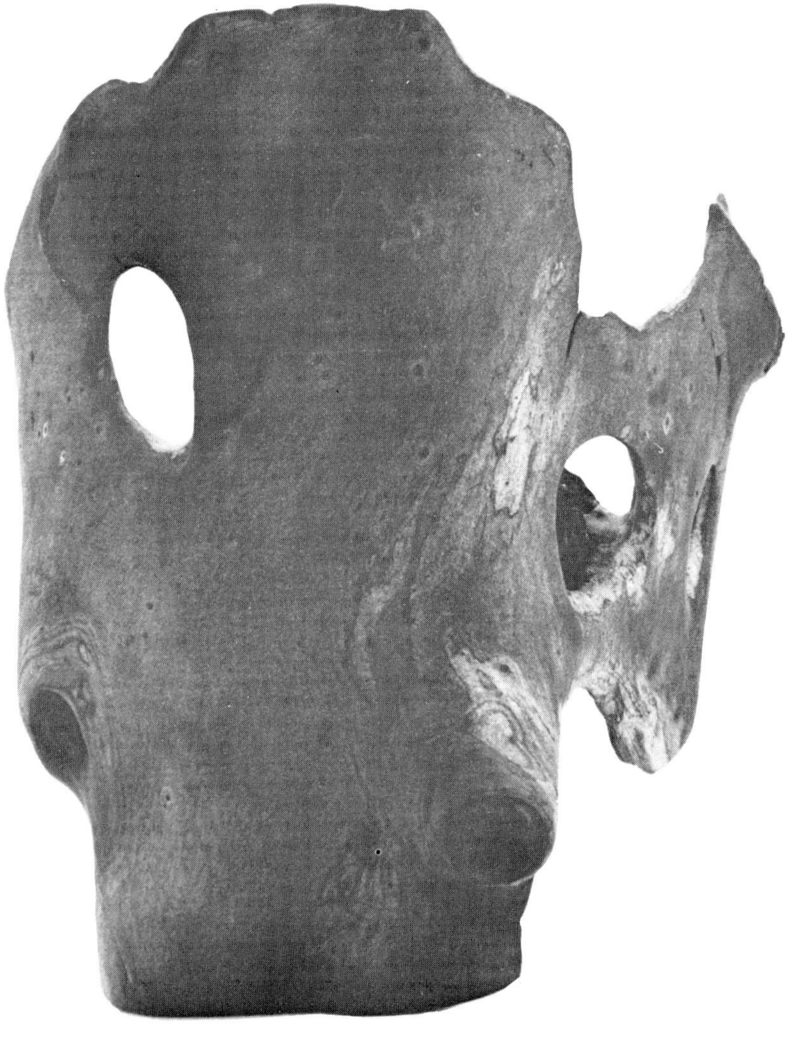

41 'Holy Man' was the end result of controlled burn that nearly got out of control. Originally it was a larger section from a driftwood log. A large part of the interior and about half of the cylindrical outside literally went up in smoke. Fire came through the surface in many places; the idea of a mask came just in time and the burning of the harder shell was stopped. With so many holes in it, it just had to be 'Holy Man'; it was made as a wall hanging.

9 Finishes

Trees in bloom are a wonderful sight and most people cannot fail to be moved by them. But the beautiful blossom, radiant in all its colours, is a fragile and transient thing. After a few short weeks it falls and lies blowing in the wind. There is, however, a more durable beauty in the colours which lie hidden deep in the grain of the tree itself. When these colours are seen by human eyes it is usually in the fine finish and grain of a piece of good furniture. Seldom is it associated with the hidden colours deep within the growing tree until you see them glowing in the intricate shapes of a driftwood sculpture.

The drying and seasoning of wood causes the colours to become dull and drab, but they can be easily restored in furniture or driftwood by applying a suitable finish. There are quite a number of products to choose from, some of which also seal the surface and help to protect your work. When carefully applied they will emphasize the wood-grain patterns and produce highlights that add lustre, life and sparkle to your sculptures.

Surface preparation

Before starting to apply any finish it is important to make certain that the surface is smooth, dry and free from dust and grease. This is where sandpaper comes into its own. To use it does not require much skill but it does need a sustained and patient effort. Having got the best possible surface with the use of tools, careful sanding is the key to a professional-looking finish.

Start sandpapering lightly and evenly, working in the direction of the grain and using only as coarse a grade as is necessary; a grade that is too coarse will only score the surface and make it worse. The process is repeated again and again, each time using progressively finer grades of sandpaper until you achieve a satisfying, satin-smooth finish. The job can be tedious but it is one of the hallmarks of good craftsmanship, and the results of whatever finishing coats you decide to apply will depend on it.

When you encounter areas that are difficult to get at the sandpaper can be torn into long, thin strips and pulled backwards and forwards round curves or through holes, for example. In situations where this is impossible, wind a strip around a stick to twirl it in a cavity or crevice. With driftwood straightforward, flat surfaces are the

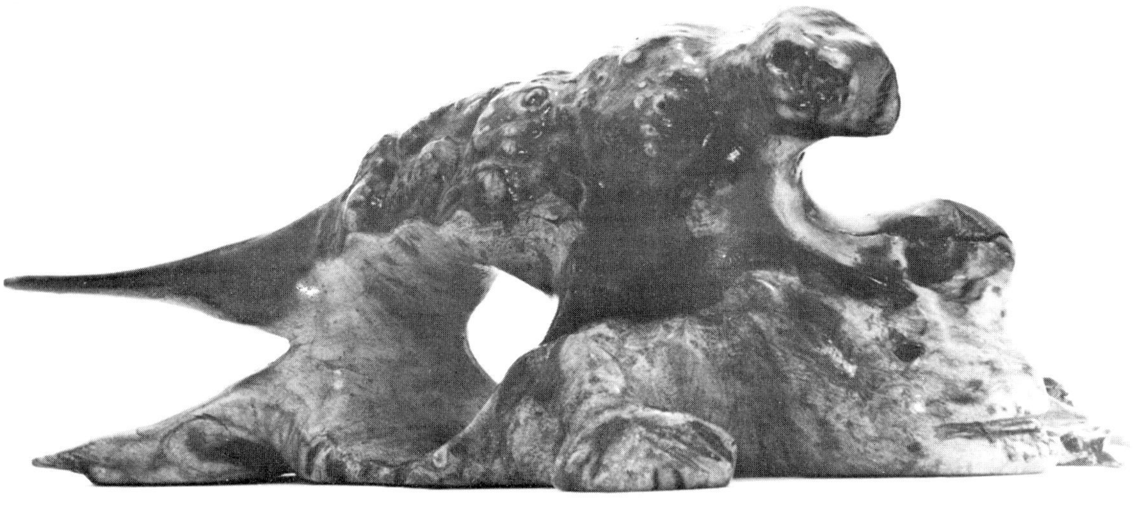

42 This 'Beast to Guard Treasure' was made from the piece of driftwood remaining below the A—B line in plate 39. The tail piece was shortened and a vee-shaped piece cut into it to give the double tail effect. The large hole through the centre was made to reduce its otherwise chunky appearance and to add interest. Rich colours and textures abound, and these were emphasized by three coats of a clear, matt polyurethane varnish. (Perhaps his treasure will be lying on the strand-line after the next tide!)

exception, so be prepared to improvise. When all sanding is finished make sure all the dust is brushed and blown away.

When it comes to the actual finishing coats check the manufacturer's instructions. Use brushes which will not shed their hairs and cloths which will not lint or leave fluff. It would be a shame to spoil the ship for a ha'porth of tar.

Stains and dyes

These can be spirit-based, water-based or in powder form. The spirit-based varieties work well with all woods and are readily available at most DIY and hardware stores. They come in a wide range of colours, from light pine and maple to the darkest ebony. If a driftwood sculpture lacks colour, or if spotting, touching-in or a full contrast is needed there are natural wood shades for every purpose.

Stains and dyes are very strong and may need to be diluted. Always make tests on scrap pieces of similar wood before using on the main work. An evenly applied coverage is important or patchiness will occur: staining may be an end in itself, or may be followed by some form of polishing.

Oil- and wax-based polishes

The traditional wood waxes are beeswax (animal), cornuba wax (vegetable) and paraffin wax (mineral). These are tough, hard and tallow-like at normal temperatures and need some form of gentle heat to soften them; not over a naked flame, as they are inflammable. Linseed oil can be used for a natural oiled finish. An old and well-

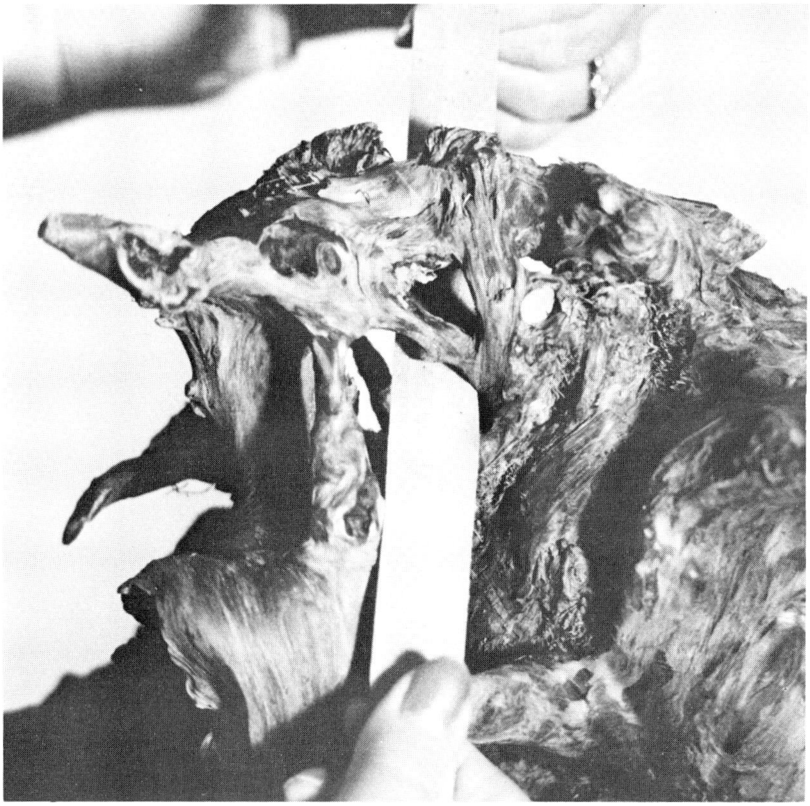

43 A good sculpture can have a mixture of surface textures, from superfine where bark has been removed to very coarse where it has been left on, and may include other distinctive features such as natural breaks or splits. One thing all surfaces have in common is the need for smoothness. There should be no splinters, spikes, sharp cutting edges or any other danger to hands. The sculpture being made here has many intricate natural shapes with places where fingers cannot reach, so strips of sandpaper were pulled to and fro, and where this was not possible small files were used for smoothing. The main requirement for this sort of job is patience.

tried medium for polishing is beeswax dissolved in turpentine, with which it can be reduced to any consistency, even down to a liquid.

Whether using waxes or oils always allow time for the medium to penetrate the wood, using brushes to work it well into the surface. Follow with plenty of dry, light brushing and buffing with clean cloths.

The wide variety of domestic polishes available do provide quicker and more convenient alternatives. Aerosol sprays can of course be used, but additional coats will be needed; polishes containing silicones give a more durable finish.

Spirit-based polishes

These include button, and French polish and others based on shellac and natural resins. Traditional ways of raising a hard finish and high gloss, these are specialist polishes requiring skilful and patient application. They are good on hard, flat surfaces but difficult to apply to uneven, indented areas. Shellac is refined from a natural resin secreted by the female Lac insect (*Coccus lacca*). The polish can be made by dissolving one part shellac in three or four parts of methylated spirit.

Paint and lacquer

It may sound like sacrilege to consider painting driftwood sculptures. Mention of it is made here because some very unusual, strong effects can be achieved with black or white matt finishes, or with gold or silver lacquers. These can have considerable impact when used with specialist lighting and floral displays for exhibition purposes.

Varnishes

Traditional varnishes are gradually being superseded by modern polyurethane types, which do give excellent results. These are very easy to use, they have good penetration, seal the surface and are quick-drying. Apart from a wide range of matt satin and gloss finishes there are others which incorporate wood colouring agents. They give a tough, protective coating to all kinds of driftwood textures, which makes them ideal for many kinds of sculptures.

Acrylics

Under this broad heading is another group of modern materials which can be of use to the driftwood sculptor. It includes a wide range of artist's colours and glazes, which can be diluted with water to give only the slightest hint of glaze or colour or used undiluted for intense colour and high gloss. They are quick-drying and give a tough, durable finish which is waterproof, does not crack or shrink and can be used on most types of surface. Acrylic pastes can be used with many inert substances to make 'fillers' or by themselves as adhesives. If you like to experiment here are versatile materials with many known uses, and probably plenty more waiting to be discovered.

Preservatives

Solid, well-seasoned driftwood is not likely to need any treatment with preservatives if other finishes are going to be applied. However, when the timber has been tunnelled and colonized by marine life, or has open grain and cleavages, some form of preservative may be advisable. Although there are many types on the market, choice is best restricted to colourless varieties that do not have a lingering odour and can be safely polished or glazed afterwards.

Protection out of doors

Not all sculptures are house-bound. Some like to live permanently outside. They may stand guard by your door, or on a pillar by the gate or make a focal point in the garden. In these situations, and provided that no other finishing is planned, they can be given a protective coat of creosote. This will also have a colouring effect; it is usually sold in shades of brown, ranging from light golden to dark. Although it is very effective for outdoor use the smell lingers on for several weeks, and it should also be kept away from plants.

There is an ever-increasing range of coverings, coatings and protective finishes on the market. You can go from a humble tin of shoe polish to a complete encapsulation in clear plastic resin. Every driftwood sculpture that you make is the product of your own creative originality. If you have new ideas for finishes, have fun trying them.

10 Other useful finds

Unidentified objects

'Seek and ye shall find' is certainly true of driftwood hunting expeditions, and you will frequently find much more besides. Everyone hopes to discover gold ducats or pieces of eight washed up from some sunken treasure ship, and just now and again someone does make a rare find like this. But the sea does not yield its secrets easily. After years or centuries on the sea bed, when such treasures do come ashore they are for the most part unrecognizable: discoloured, battered, encrusted with scale and secretion, covered in sand and seaweed – not at all what you may expect. They need specialist cleaning and restoring before they resemble the treasure you see in a museum.

Recently a holidaymaker on a Devon beach found what she thought was a piece of old corroded wire; it turned out to be a gold Viking bracelet worth several thousand pounds. All this just goes to show that it pays to look carefully at the things you find on beaches.

Look, but in some cases where unidentified objects are found, definitely do not touch! This warning refers to the occasionally dangerous things which do come ashore from time to time, perhaps in large quantities, after gales and shipwreck.

While most people could recognize lethal weapons like rockets, torpedoes and similar military hardware, other hazards may be much less obvious. Beware if you should ever find a beach strewn with packages, boxes, canisters, etc. They may contain toxic chemicals, acids, industrial poisons or all manner of harmful substances, washed overboard from a ship's deck cargo. Fortunately these occurrences are rare, and for the most part the beach is a happy holiday place, but if you do see anything which looks suspicious, alert the local police.

On the days when there are no gold ducats or torpedoes lying around, which is probably more than 99 per cent of the time, if you can spare a thought for things other than driftwood the beach has other free 'art material' to offer, things that, with a little ingenuity and imagination, can be combined with driftwood to lend another dimension to your sculptures. Some are natural products of the sea while others are man-made objects which the sea has changed.

Shells

The beauty of shells is well known, and much has been written on the subject of making things with them. Usually bright and colourful, they possess a dominance in their own right which is quick to clash with a driftwood sculpture. Avoid the temptation to encrust a sculpture with scores of little pearly shells as if it were a cheap gift box. If you are expressing a theme and feel that shells help to convey the message, it is better to use a single shell dramatically and poignantly, like a rose in a specimen vase. Whatever kind you choose, make sure that it helps your driftwood sculpture to tell its story; let it be noticed but not steal the limelight.

Fossils

Fossils, whether plant or animal, are not easily found or identified, which makes it all the more interesting if you do happen to discover one. Of marine species, the trilobites and ammonites are perhaps the best known, and finds of the latter have varied in size from the diameter of a small watch to that of a large cartwheel.

As far as driftwood sculptures are concerned, a recognizable fossil such as an ammonite provides a compelling point of interest in the overall design. The two media can work together in harmony but neither is dependent on the other. Many would say that a fossil is just an inanimate object like a stone which tabulates a period of time on the geological calendar of the earth's evolution. But there is another, deeper way of seeing a fossil.

Take a fossil to a quiet place where you can sit for a while in contemplation. It is a revealing experience to reflect on this life, which was lived more than one hundred million years ago. Turned to stone and now cradled in your hand is a very tangible link with the earth's distant past. As you are now living your life, this creature also lived its span on the same planet. It lived when time still had many more millions of years to run before the earliest primitive man-like creatures evolved. Could an even stranger creature hold and contemplate your fossilized remains one hundred million years from now?

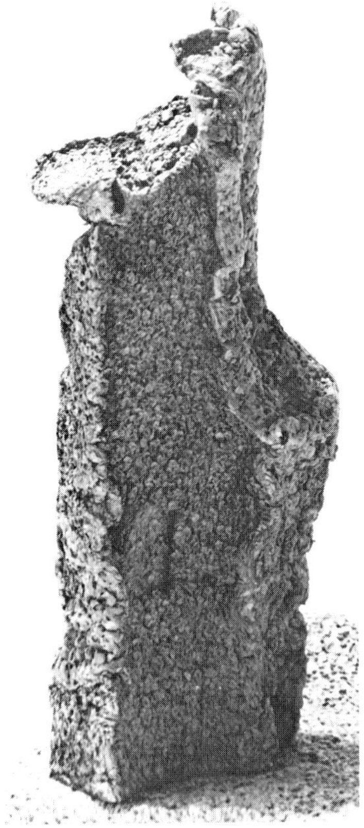

44 *Already standing on its own as a monument to man's abuse of his environment, this piece of drift-plastic owes its transformation to nature. In the sea it has acquired a new character, with subtle colours and strong textures. Now compatible with driftwood, it can help you in expressing stories, themes and idea in an unusual and effective way.*

Polystyrene and other plastics

Much has been said and written about pollution by man of his own environment, but the lakes, rivers and seas are still being used as the world's dustbins. In spite of the great efforts of conservation groups and the more aware governments a lot of this rubbish still finds its way on to the strand-line of our beaches.

Nature's army of marine workers can, as already mentioned, cope with natural substances like wood, and there is now evidence that they are trying to adapt to man-made products, which are much more

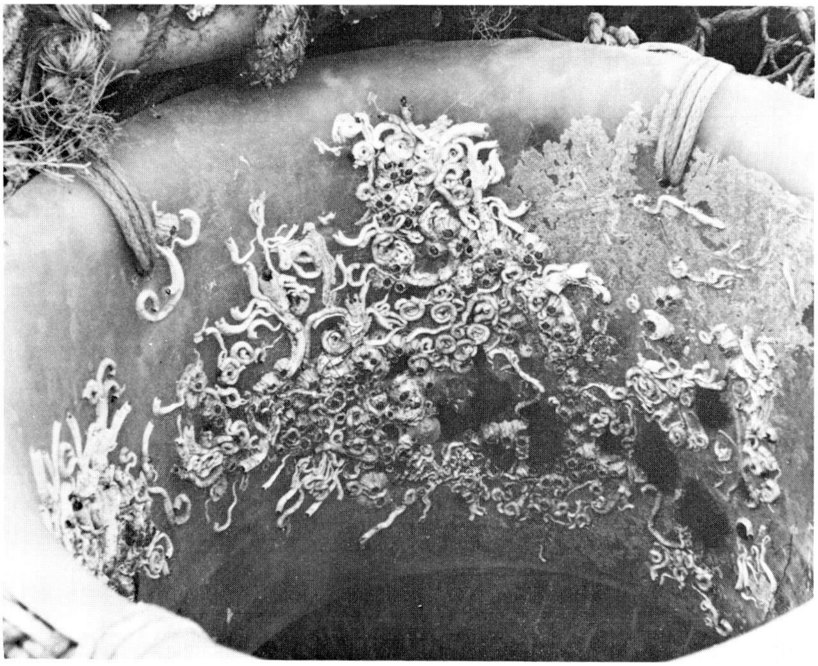

45 This is the top of an old crabpot which came out of the sea prettier than when it went in. The plastic rim has been colonized by barnacles and delicately patterned with marine encrustations. How you use things like this in conjunction with driftwood sculpture is part of the challenge. Of course you do not have to use the whole pot: you could cut out small patterned sections with a fretsaw and let ideas blossom.

durable. Plastics, in particular (and some of the tougher varieties were once thought to be virtually indestructible in sea water), can be found covered with marine encrustations. It is almost as if, lacking the ability to break down or digest them, nature's workers are in desperation trying to camouflage, to colonize or just to beautify these alien substances that have invaded their environment. (Think for a moment what a great scream would go up from the human race if aliens from outer space decided to chuck all their rubbish into man's living space on his part of this planet, particularly if some of it was highly toxic and killed off whole sections of the populace!) To the collector of driftwood nature's efforts with plastics can mean some interesting and unusual finds, which can be incorporated into his own creative schemes. Examples of modern 'drift-plastic' are shown in plates 44 and 45.

Polystyrene, while by no means indestructible, does take a lot of breaking down. Lighter and more buoyant than cork, it travels long distances driven by the wind and carried on the ocean currents. In heavy seas, which break up tougher and more solid objects, polystyrene skips along the surface, escaping much of the impact; in high winds it leaves the crest of a breaking wave and 'flies' over the surface. But it does change in some interesting ways.

The piece shown in plate 44 was originally smooth and white like any other piece normally used for packaging. Now the square edges have been changed into weathered curves and folds and the surface has taken on several different textures. Some parts are like smooth stone pebbles, others are honeycombed, while yet another area has distinct fish-like scales. Much of the surface has the look and feel of a crunchy biscuit, interspersed here and there with little outcrops which have a wood-grain appearance. Gone, too, is the drab white colour of polystyrene; it is now alive with pleasing shades of fawn, brown, orange and amber. How long this piece had been in the sea is not known but the curious shapes, textures and colours it acquired there created a pleasing transformation.

Glass

There is an element of romance and mystery about finding a corked bottle on the beach. As soon as your eye sees the cork the mind flashes the question 'Is there a message in it?' and you look, expecting to find one.

Messages in bottles have been around as long as bottles themselves. They have always excited public imagination and aroused speculation, in England perhaps never more so than in the reign of Queen Elizabeth I, when these matters really came to a head. In the year 1560 she appointed an official 'uncorker of bottles' following an incident in which important state secrets had been found washed ashore in a bottle. It was decreed that unauthorized persons caught opening bottles cast up by the sea should be hanged. This state of affairs lasted for over two hundred years until the time of George III, such was the concern about messages. But what about the bottles, what happened to them?

Bottles were much scarcer in the sixteenth century and they would doubtless have been kept for reuse; today we live in a throwaway society, so who cares about a bottle? Well, perhaps a driftwood sculptor might care, or a conservationist, or an angry parent whose child has just suffered a badly gashed foot and is desperately applying first aid. It is a sad fact that many people just do not care about bottles in the sea and the hazards of broken glass along the shore.

In due time surf and sand will smooth away the sharp edges, and dangerous bottles become interesting fragments of coloured glass – interesting, that is, to a driftwood sculptor because they can be incorporated into his work. They could be used 'window fashion' either in or between suitable areas, or you might wish to give a green eye to a little yellow god; other creations may need glass 'eyes' as well – 'Beast to Guard Treasure' (plate 42), for example. There is scope for using glass as a linking feature, or alternatively to divide or contain the action within parts that comprise a sculpture. Another way of using glass is to create small mosaic patterns on appropriately flat surfaces, or to make a little inlay, work that will create a focal point.

Mounting glass into a driftwood sculpture can be accomplished with the aid of modelling materials such as the cold-setting clay types. These lend themselves to easy shaping and moulding and can be made to blend in naturally with driftwood shapes and textures. The material can be coloured before being used or touched in with acrylic paints after it has dried to make the mounts indistinguishable. The object of using glass should not be to try to gild the lily or turn the work into a montage. Its purpose is to give little glints and reflections, to catch and hold the stray shaft of sunlight, not to turn the thing into a kaleidoscope.

Glass ground smooth by the action of sea and sand loses some of its transparency and becomes frosted and opaque. A coat of clear varnish is all that is needed to brighten up the surface; sea-worn glass treated in this way gives the glow of light without the glitter and is more in keeping with the mellowness of driftwood.

Perhaps if a law was introduced to hang people caught throwing glass bottles into the sea for the next two hundred years, in the twenty-third century your driftwood sculptures incorporating genuine 'sea-glass' would be even more rare and valuable collector's items.

Mermaid's purse

This popular local name sounds much more romantic than calling it the egg sac of the dogfish, which is what a mermaid's purse really is. A bit longer and thicker than a man's finger, they have four pointed corners from which long nylon-like strings are attached. These serve as anchor cables to fasten the egg sac to the seaweed. Translucent, dark grey-green or grey-brown in colour, the purses are made from a gelatinous-like substance which is surprisingly thick and tough. They can be found washed up along the strand-line after the young fish have hatched in the early months of the year.

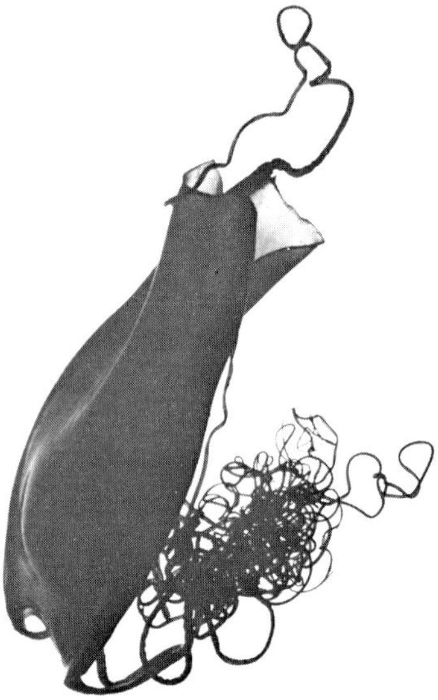

46 What keeps the mermaid in her purse?
A lure for a sailor, or something worse?
No! she likes the same as all the girls,
A mirror, a comb and a string of pearls.

If you want to find a mermaid's purse look closely among the tangled seaweed along the strand-line in the early months of the year.

Exposed to the air the purses dry, shrivel and lose their shape. If you wish to preserve them for use with a driftwood sculpture it is necessary to control the drying-out process. This can be done by filling the empty purse with fine sand and letting it dry out only very slowly, in a cool, moist, shady place to begin with, acclimatizing it gradually to drier conditions. When properly dry, glazing with a clear polyurethane will seal the surface and restore the shine.

When and where to use a mermaid's purse has to be left to the discretion of the driftwood sculptor and considered with the theme he is pursuing. Obviously no self-respecting mermaid should be without her purse and these curious little objects can only add to the overall fascination of the finished sculpture (see plate 54).

Cork

This responds beautifully to being in the sea and weathers into some very interesting shapes. It is a pleasant and easy material to work with. Because of its exceptional buoyancy and light weight it is usually to be found on the highest limits of the tide-line. Once widely used by fishermen, it is now being replaced by the use of plastic and is not so easy to find as it used to be. In the sculpture 'Nautilus' (see plate 35) a piece of cork was used for the base, a purpose for which it is ideal.

Cordage

Pieces of rope and line are nearly always lying around on beaches; they can be woven, plaited or coiled, and when fastened onto a firm surface they make effective textured baseboards. Cordage made from natural fibres takes colour and varnish well; man-made fibres with less 'cling' would require acrylic finishes. Short lengths of rope whipped at one end and unstranded at the other can create the effect of a sea anemone.

Cuttle 'bones'

The flat white oval cuttle 'bones' are the internal shells of cuttle fish,

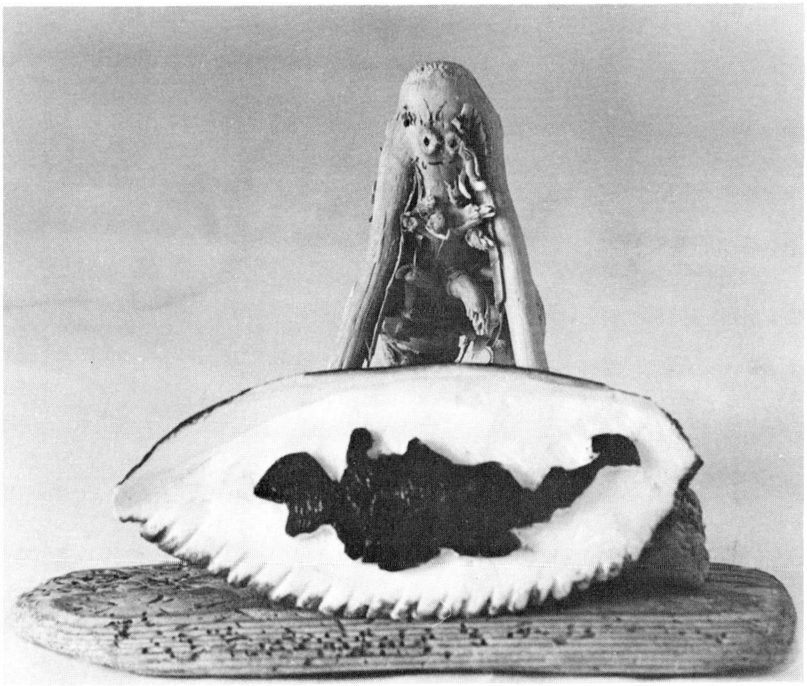

47 Meet Professor Cuttle-Carver! The Professor holds his audience enthralled as he lectures on 'Carving the cuttle'. He strongly recommends that anyone who has not tried carving this medium should do so at the first opportunity. The cuttle bone is so firm and yet carves so easily that it is sheer joy to work with. Pencil a design on the surface, cut round it with a thin, sharp stencil knife and pare away the surplus from around the cut outline.

which come close inshore in early summer to spawn. They favour sheltered, sandy regions and in these shallower waters many seem to perish; after a strong gale a beach may be strewn with hundreds of these cuttle bones. The cuttle bone is firm and yet very easy to cut and carve, readily lending itself to use with driftwood sculptures, bas-relief name plates, etc.

A bag of bones

Beachcombing is always interesting and full of surprises. You can go out looking for driftwood and find Viking gold, or just come back home with a bag full of old bones – like those in plate 48. So what's special about bones? Even a dog would not want these! For a start, they were there, spread along the strand-line one after the other; you could not help seeing them. You don't usually find bones on the beach, at least not ones like these – old, well washed, with beautiful textures; and because driftwood makes you curious, you find your curiosity spilling over onto bones, and you speculate . . .

Everyone likes a wishbone; they are lucky, a talisman to bring you good fortune, to make a wish come true. 'I am going to be lucky, I can feel it in my bones.' 'The trouble with you lazy-bones is that you are bone idle.' 'Not so fast, bone-head, I've a bone to pick with you!' 'If you talk to me like that I'll break every bone in your body!'

So you see the subject is not as dry as a bone, it can be very interesting, these are bones of contention, every one! They make

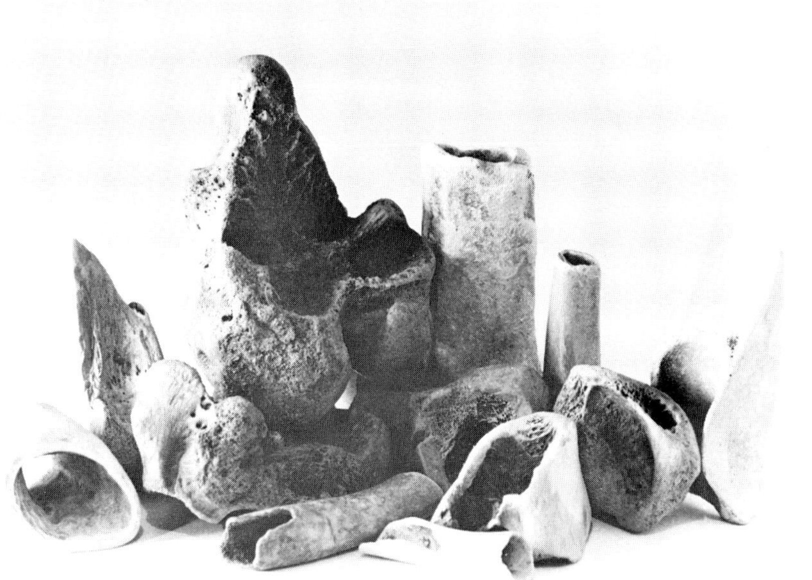

48 These old bones were scattered along a beach where driftwood was being collected. They were clean, weather-worn and full of interesting shapes, colours and textures; more importantly, they proved to be compatible with driftwood. The large bone in the centre was used as a base in 'Epitaph to a Seabird' (see plate 54).

people react emotionally. So the idea occurs, will they go with a driftwood sculpture to assist in expressing a theme? And the answer is, yes they will! Ways of using driftwood sculptures to make strong visual statements are discussed later. Meanwhile anything which adds to their impact deserves consideration; make no bones about it, they can be used with considerable effect.

In plate 49, 'Egyptian Storyteller', the seated 'boy' is a sea-worn bone, used as found.

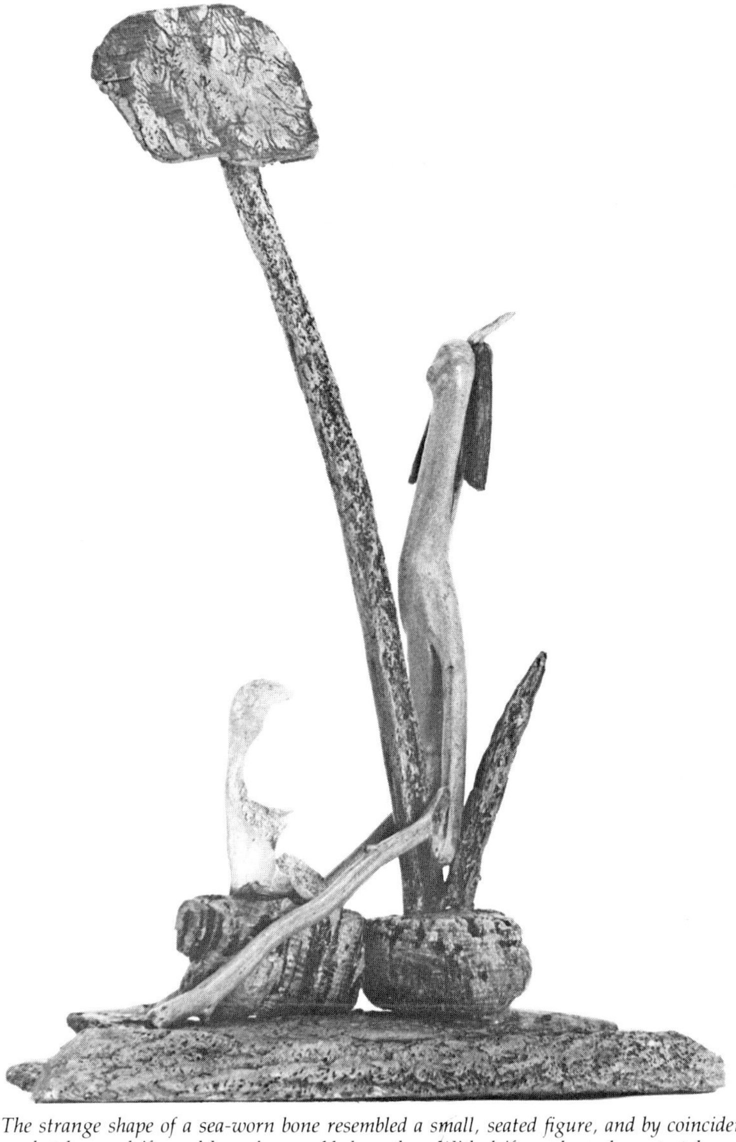

49 The strange shape of a sea-worn bone resembled a small, seated figure, and by coincidence a somewhat larger driftwood branch resembled another. With driftwood you learn to take things as they come; if today is going to be the day for finding seated figures, then so be it! The idea was pursued further, and when some distinctly Ancient Egyptian features were observed, they were emphasized by cutting and carving. The result was the 'Egyptian Storyteller' pictured here.

Before leaving the subject of other finds it may be prudent briefly to draw attention to the law, which says that if no rightful owner can be found, valuables washed up on the beach traditionally belong to the Crown and should be reported to the Receiver of Wrecks at the Department of Customs and Excise. So do not regard it as a case of 'finder's keepers' for the ancient gold and jewels that you find until it has been cleared by the gentlemen at the Department, though it is the practice nowadays to return them to the finder, or, if they are required by a national museum for historical reasons, to reimburse the finder with the current market value.

Sea-bed drifters

When you start looking for other objects it soon becomes apparent what a lot of other things there are around on our beaches. If some of these have been in the sea for centuries, or in the case of fossils for untold millions of years, others are relative newcomers. Some of the newest of all are the sea-bed drifters – see plate 50.

Woodhead sea-bed drifters are specially designed and used to plot the currents which flow just above the sea bed, hence their name. They are released into the sea at known locations by the scientists at the Ministry of Agriculture and Fisheries, and a reward is offered to the finders who return their identity tags to the research laboratory at Lowestoft. In this way the scientists gain valuable information which helps them in their plotting of the patterns of fish migration. The drifter shown in the photograph had taken almost three years to travel from its release point off the Yorkshire coast to its recovery point on a beach near Torquay in Devon. Life is full of interesting surprises for the driftwood sculptor!

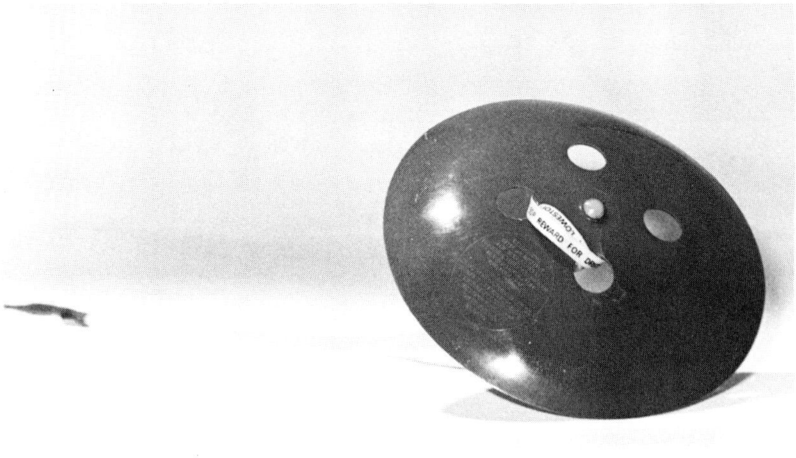

50 Over the last twenty years more than thirty thousand of these sea-bed drifters have been released around the coasts of Great Britain. Approximately 50 per cent are found and returned to the Fisheries Laboratory within a year of their release. The finders receive a (modest) reward and the scientists learn more about currents in the sea and the way these affect the lives and stocks of fish.

11 *Driftwood sculpture and flowers*

The use of driftwood in flower arranging is an old and well established practice, but like so many ancient arts its origin is lost in antiquity. It is debatable whether the first primitive woman to practise the art gathered flowers and embellished them with a piece of driftwood; or whether she had a piece of driftwood and embellished this with a flower. Driftwood sculptors no doubt favour the latter theory, maintaining that the woman would probably have been sent out to gather wood to keep the camp fire going through the night. There would probably have been driftwood among her fuel; finding this just too pretty to burn she stood it on the ground by the side of her bed of rushes. That night when she went to bed she hung the garland of flowers from about her neck on the driftwood 'flower stand'.

If this sounds like a fairy story, it is! Even more surprising is that this incident was almost equally certain to have been the first of many stages which have now culminated in all the appurtenances of the modern boudoir. It simply goes to show that there is an enduring relationship between driftwood, flowers and people which has spanned the centuries. The simple truth of the matter is that all three species like each other and get on well together.

This chapter seeks to further that relationship and to explore ways in which floral artistry can use driftwood sculptures in place of the random bits of driftwood so frequently employed in the past. The object is to bring these two art forms together in such a way that neither one is diminished and both contribute to widen the creative scope for artistic expression. In carefully thought out and well balanced arrangements such combinations command attention because of their originality. They make an irresistible partnership which cannot be ignored.

Dominance and design

By now you will have accepted the fact that a driftwood sculpture is a very dominant creature. It is probably true to say that it controlled and guided your actions from the moment that you found the wild wood on the strand-line. Was it not its own inbuilt characteristics which led you to fashion its current form? So when combining it with floral art, do not be surprised to find that it is still calling the tune and still guiding the pattern of your creative urges.

It is this dominance which needs to be understood; it is not just because it is made of wood, or is more solid, or has a strong linear appeal, or for any other physical reason. The dominance lies in the reaction that humans have to it – a little bit of magic fascination which cannot be ignored. Once you have recognized this and reconciled yourself to it, your efforts will be all the more rewarding.

With any good design the scale, proportions and balance of the components need to be in harmony, so the first thing to decide is which of your driftwood sculptures you are going to use. This could well be your last free decision, because from here almost everything else that happens will be influenced by it.

The size of the sculpture you choose is very important because this will control the ultimate size of the finished arrangement. While a small sculpture can maintain its own appeal and still complement

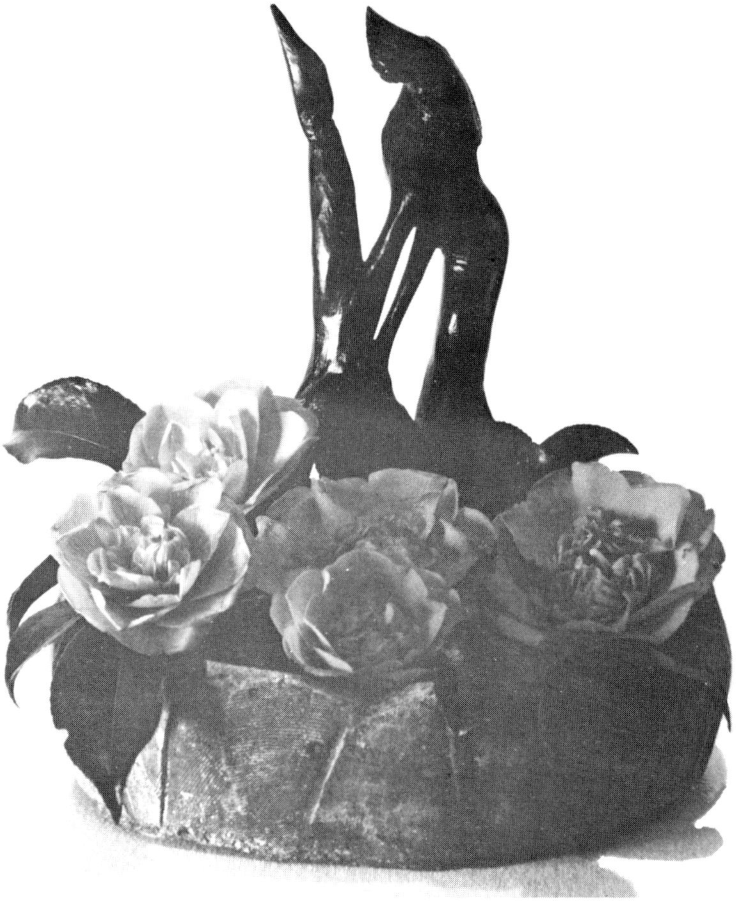

51 *A stone bowl with flowers floating on the water is a fairly commonplace arrangement. It is usually accompanied by a small gnome or a boy fishing. What makes this so very different is the sculpture. Those who see it are usually astonished to discover that it is called 'Penguinity' and is made from driftwood (see also plate 19).*

quite a large floral display, its proportions do have to relate to the overall design. A sculpture which is too big cannot be cut down to size by sawing a bit off, as you would if it were just a random piece of driftwood. Trying to hide part of it among the leaves and flowers does not work either. Such is the power to incite curiosity that in no time at all curious fingers would be probing to expose it, to the detriment of the arrangement as a whole.

If you do want to use a large sculpture but do not have the space to accommodate an equally large finished display keep the flowers few and simple. Go to the extreme if you must and use a single well-chosen bloom. The effect can be very dramatic and is a powerful way of expressing an emotional theme. Once you have set the basic pattern from the sculpture's own size and configuration, select leaf and flower sizes which also help to create good balance.

Before the enjoyable work of floral arranging can begin, it is essential to provide a strong, stable base to which everything can be firmly fixed. Apart from giving structural stability, it should also be of the right size and shape to complement the design. When you are considering scale, proportion and balance, spare a thought for the ultimate display area. Get the basics right and the rest will be real pleasure.

A base for construction

If the driftwood sculpture has a baseboard of its own which is large enough to accommodate flower holders, water containers and the materials to screen them from view, then this can of course be used. There are, however, limitations to taking this simple course. It would be all too easy to destroy the sculptural effect by crowding the base with bric-à-brac. Then there would be an added restriction on the siting of these holders and containers, which should of course be strategically placed so that they may be concealed or camouflaged. Alternatively, if they are themselves of an artistic nature, they could not be displayed to their own best advantage in a limited space. But the best reason of all for not using the sculpture's own base is that this avoids its being damaged by scuffing and scratching.

A sound base for construction and on which the sculpture will also stand can be made from a variety of materials. An obvious choice would be a larger piece of driftwood with a flat, reasonably level surface. The shape could be any which seems appropriate, and although much of the surface will not be seen in the finished display it will need some working and finishing. A timber base, except one made from the hardest kinds of wood, is an easy base on which to fasten things with pins, tacks and nails.

Sheets of metal and glass, mirrors, large china or earthenware dishes, glass fruit bowls and kitchen trays all get pressed into service for flower arrangements. But these do present problems when firm fixings are required for flower holders and water containers. While these items may be satisfactory for flower displays using the odd driftwood branch in the traditional way, a driftwood sculpture may seem ill at ease in an antique soup tureen, for example. They like to be out in the open with space around them.

One material which has much to recommend it as a base in floral–sculpture work is dense quality polystyrene. This can be obtained in sheets about as thick as two fingers, or even three or four if you wish. Its very cheapness and versatility has made it one of the modern world's throwaway packaging materials, with a thousand and one other uses; by using it for our bases we make it one thousand and two. If there is none being thrown away in your locality at the moment, you can buy it at your local hobby shop. So easily is it cut, carved or sliced by a sharp knife that working with it is a real joy, as you will soon discover.

It does not have to remain the formal geometrical rectangle or square that you bought in the shop. It can be transformed into a flower or leaf shape or whatever you choose, simply by drawing or tracing on the surface with a ballpoint pen and cutting along the outline. The same technique can be used to mark and cut out a recess into which the driftwood sculpture's own base will fit neatly. Containers for water and flower holders can be similarly bedded into the polystyrene. Should any kind of supporting floral framework be needed, such as bamboo or wires, the ends can be firmly anchored by pushing them directly into it.

If the need arises, polystyrene can be worked and 'carved' with a hot soldering iron or similar tool. A word of warning: toxic fumes are given off and these must not be inhaled. This sort of work should be done out of doors, where the fumes can quickly disperse. Polystyrene sheet is normally white, which is not the best colour for a base, and it will therefore need a coat of matt emulsion paint to subdue its starkness. The choice of colour will depend upon your individual creation.

Incorporating driftwood sculptures into floral arrangements does not require special techniques. The artistic skills are already in the hands of the floral arranger; but let there also be sympathetic tolerance and understanding for the vagaries of this wayward medium. Because there are so many good books available which cover the subject of flower arranging in great detail, the only other suggestions offered here are concerned with PPDS – the Protection and Preservation of Driftwood Sculptures.

Short of some great natural calamity, like earthquake, fire or flood, a well-made driftwood sculpture may well outlast you, provided that you and the rest of the human race treats it fairly. So please consider, and try to abide by, the following code of practice.

If you do not wish your carefully fashioned sculpture to revert to its wild state, keep it out of water. Flowers do need water so that their fragile lives may be prolonged for a few more days; provide this in good measure, but in such a way that your driftwood sculpture remains dry. Although the odd gentle spraying, at a flower show for example, will not unduly harm it, it could of course temporarily be covered or removed. Flowers and foliage frequently need a framework, and wood is a very handy substance on which to fasten them. Resist the temptation to pin, clip, nail, tie, stick or screw anything on to your sculpture. Once in a while give it a little overhaul; it does not take much, just brush away any dust and give it a bit of a polish and a rub up. This shows that you really care, and when your displays are finished and the last petal has fallen the sculpture, still in prime condition, will be ready to help you again and again.

Presentation and display

Driftwood sculptures and floral arrangements provide wonderful media for self expression, and the pleasure of making them is accompanied by a measure of peace and contentment. This is just one of those little things in life which money can't buy; it is a door through which you can escape from stress and tension into the wonderland of your own creative imagination. But satisfying your own creative needs can be extended to bring pleasure to other people if they can see and enjoy your work as well. Showing your work to the best advantage is the culmination of all your efforts, and it is only when it is placed in a situation where it is in harmony with its surroundings that you can consider your work to be finished.

Space is an important aspect of this; too little or too much can be equally distracting. The term 'space' is used here in relation to room size and the shape and form of other adjacent objects which could so easily distract the eye from your display. If there is too much space this in itself will be the detractor because your work could be engulfed by it.

Backgrounds need careful scrutiny to make sure they work in your favour. Tradition might say that a neutral background is best: a soft grey, for example, would be quite safe and never steal the show. But they do not have to be grey and neutral, they can be much more visually exciting when they provide harmony or contrast or help with the expression of a particular theme. Nor do you have to accept the colour of a blank wall because it just happens to be there. If you are faced with this situation and need something different regard it as the blank space at the back of a theatre stage on which you can design your own background – not by drawing or painting on the wall, but by using 'props'. Try hanging something compatible or a simple drape of material or netting, or rig a light to cast a distinctive shadow or silhouette. This is not as difficult as you might suppose; once you have a general impression of what is required ideas will soon come. Designing your own backgrounds can be very useful when you are using floral sculptures to express a theme.

Lighting

Natural lighting is influenced by the time of year, the time of day and the weather outside, and consequently is difficult to control. If it is the only source of light available try to be conscious of its limitations and use it to the best advantage. For the purpose in hand one of the most disastrous forms of natural lighting is strong direct sunlight, but the sun comes in other ways, some of which can be very effective. It dapples things, bathes them, makes pools, it streams and floods in, it comes in beams, bursts, rays and shafts, to name but a few. The thing which really counts is the way in which the available natural light is used.

Artificial light is much more adaptable and can be made to do anything you wish; such is the choice that it would be very easy to have too much light and thereby lose the effect. Again using the theatre as an analogy, in the course of one performance a wide range of special-effect lighting can be seen. Out of this the strongest and most lasting impressions often come from the simplest forms, when lights are low and the focus is on a central character. Of course you do not need all the trappings of theatre – it is quite an easy matter to arrange simple spot, back, or concealed lighting, and brightness, softness and colour can be as straightforward as changing a bulb. Consider your options and keep it simple.

12 Driftwood sculptures in the home

Choosing a name

If you are going to take a piece of wild driftwood and make it into a sculpture you can live with in your home, it should have a name. This is not a precondition, but it does make for a more harmonious relationship between those concerned. It may be that the problem has already been solved – perhaps the idea for a name occurred on that first day when you found the wild wood on the strand-line. However, if your sculpture still does not have a name, now is the time to find one. (You do not have to have a christening party, though it could be a novel excuse for one if you wish.) Just occasionally the right name may prove very elusive, but it would be unthinkable to leave a good work untitled, to be referred to as a 'something' or a 'whatnot'. Parents sometimes find difficulty in choosing names for children, but they can resort to lists of names and their meanings in books. Driftwood sculptors have no such facility, and as always with driftwood the answer must lie in your own ingenuity.

Lift your eyes from the workbench and seek the far horizons, slant your imagination in other directions. Books may hold the key – browse in natural history, mythology or the Bible. Hunt in dictionaries and encyclopedias and check with Roget's *Thesaurus* – that treasure-house of related words and the ideas they express. There is an old and well-tried secret way which says, 'Sleep with a charm of driftwood under your pillow and open your mind to the universe!' It seems to work.

Pièce de résistance

As interest in interior décor grows, glossy magazines are full of wonderful schemes for home improvement. Turning the pages will reveal those special commissions from the wealthy and the famous, and equally appealing interiors which advertise commercial products. There is a great competition to provide taste, charm, elegance and comfortable living; but having completed the furnishing another need frequently arises, and that is to make a focal point with some unusual *objet d'art*.

When looking closely to see what designers use for this purpose one occasionally sees an intriguing shape of random driftwood; hardly ever a driftwood sculpture because there are so few about. Being so unusual, they have much greater power to attract the eye and rivet the attention, and the viewer quietly undergoes a new visual experience. Observe this phenomenon for yourself by watching from a discreet distance when you elevate your own *pièce de résistance* to make a focal point in your home.

Although a driftwood sculpture can stand alone in splendid isolation, commanding attention from all who pass, it does not have to just stand there like an idle ornament. Generally speaking they like to get closer to people and become more involved with them. They may not be able to bark and wag their tails but they can make their presence felt and become members of the family.

Apart from their involvement with flowers around the house, there are other possibilities to consider; like the focal point of a dining table when you entertain friends – they always provoke comment at a party gathering. Sculptures stand well in conjunction with other features of the house, near to a table lamp or a reading lamp beside an armchair. They enliven a niche or alcove, complement an indoor pool or aquarium, or stand in quiet contemplation in the study or on the library table. In the privacy of a guest room they are almost always handled and closely scrutinized, and in this way the driftwood magic rubs off on to others. You will know this when your guests begin to talk about them later.

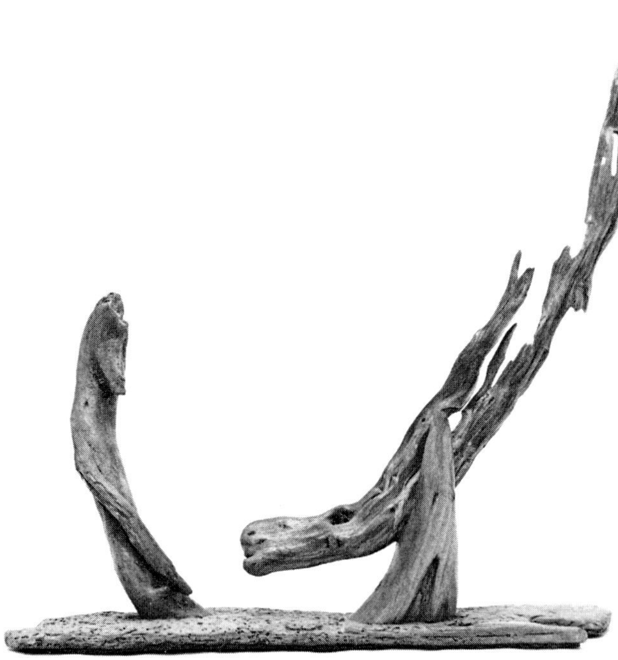

52 *'Friend of the Seahorse' (right) had been used as a model in a surrealist painting about a flight of wild horses. Later it was composed with the seahorse character (left) and mounted on a Gribble-textured base. Though it does not follow the theme of the painting, the name seemed appropriate because the two pieces went so well together.*

Driftwood sculptures really become part of the family when they are involved in leisure activities. With drawing and painting, they make admirable subjects for still-life models and hold within their strange shapes and textures innumerable ideas for abstract work. They are a designer's friend and inspiration, with a limitless supply of unusual motifs just waiting to be copied and translated into patterns for prints.

Being very photogenic, they can help the photographer in conjunction with his main subjects or as interesting background material. Two people holding and discussing a driftwood sculpture will be more at ease and make a more interesting picture than two people looking uneasily at the camera and saying 'cheese'.

Once you begin to appreciate the extent to which sculptures can contribute to your other interests they will become friends of the family. You will enjoy them much more if they have the freedom of the house!

Stories, themes and ideas

The idea of expressing a point of view without words is as old as the hills. Man must have been communicating with gestures before he could even grunt, and one of the first artifacts he used to express a point of view was probably a club. Sometimes words fail, often because of language barriers, but the gestures and artifacts still come across loud and clear: a raised, clenched fist is a defiant gesture, so beware; a raised or outspread palm is a sign of peace (but still beware). Probably a safer and more intelligent way to get your message across is with the aid of our favourite artifact, the driftwood sculpture.

One thing which is never far away from driftwood is its profound ability to spur the imagination. In addition to the floral sculpture work discussed earlier, it soon becomes apparent that there are many other materials which can be used with it to help you express stories, themes and ideas. There are basic things like stone, china, glass and marble. Some fabrics are quite compatible, as are certain metals, pewter and copper in particular. The choice is limited only by what would suit your particular theme and your imagination. If an idea sounds absurd, don't abandon it just because it may go against convention but explore it to the full, as crazy ideas are often the very fabric of originality. Old bones, eggs and candles may sound a silly mixture, but they could all three come together with a driftwood sculpture in a still-life study for an artist.

Stories, from myth and legend, from the Bible or a best-selling novel; ideas for festivals or the seasons of the year; themes from music and songs – all these invite expression by a driftwood sculptor. If you have a message burning inside you, whether it is personal, for a group or for the world at large; when you feel that you need

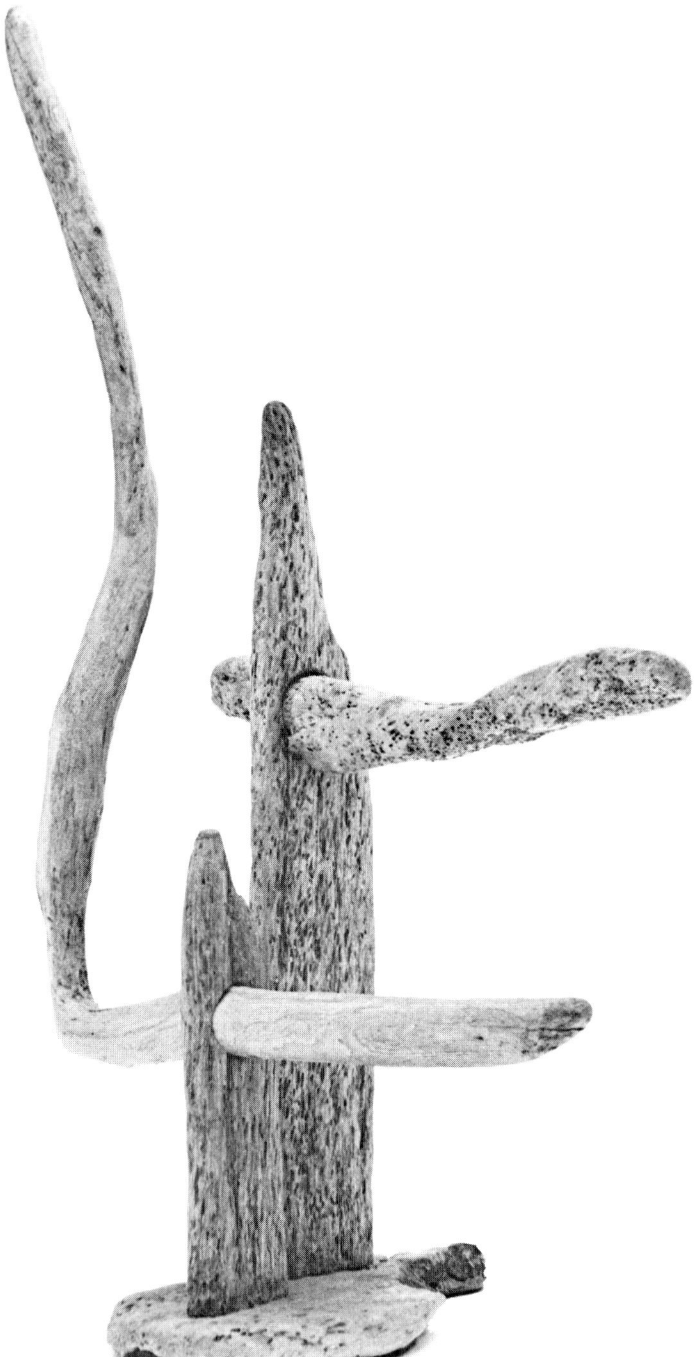

53 This sculpture is particularly dominant. It makes a very strong visual signal which in any language says 'Stop!' With much of the human race trying to persuade others to stop doing things with which they disagree, this sculpture has a universal impact in expressing themes. Entitled 'Thou Shalt Not', it would have equally strong appeal Saving the Whales or Banning the Bomb.

something more forceful than words and you are too civilized to reach for a club, let this powerful means of silent communication do it for you. Apart from the telling impact it will have on those who see it and understand your message, it will open up exciting new pathways for your creative ability to explore.

For pleasure and profit

One of the great joys of driftwood sculpture is the creative freedom it provides. It will be evident by now what a totally fascinating experience it can be to make one, and in particular how it develops creative ability and stretches the imagination.

There is, however, another aspect of this rewarding activity that deserves mention. Carefully made driftwood sculptures are always in demand and find a ready market. People the world over like unusual things, ideas count high and they will always pay well for originality. If you wish to make money from your art you will seldom be short of a customer. Once your creations are seen and handled enough of the magic will rub off on to them to make them want to buy. Just you wait and see!

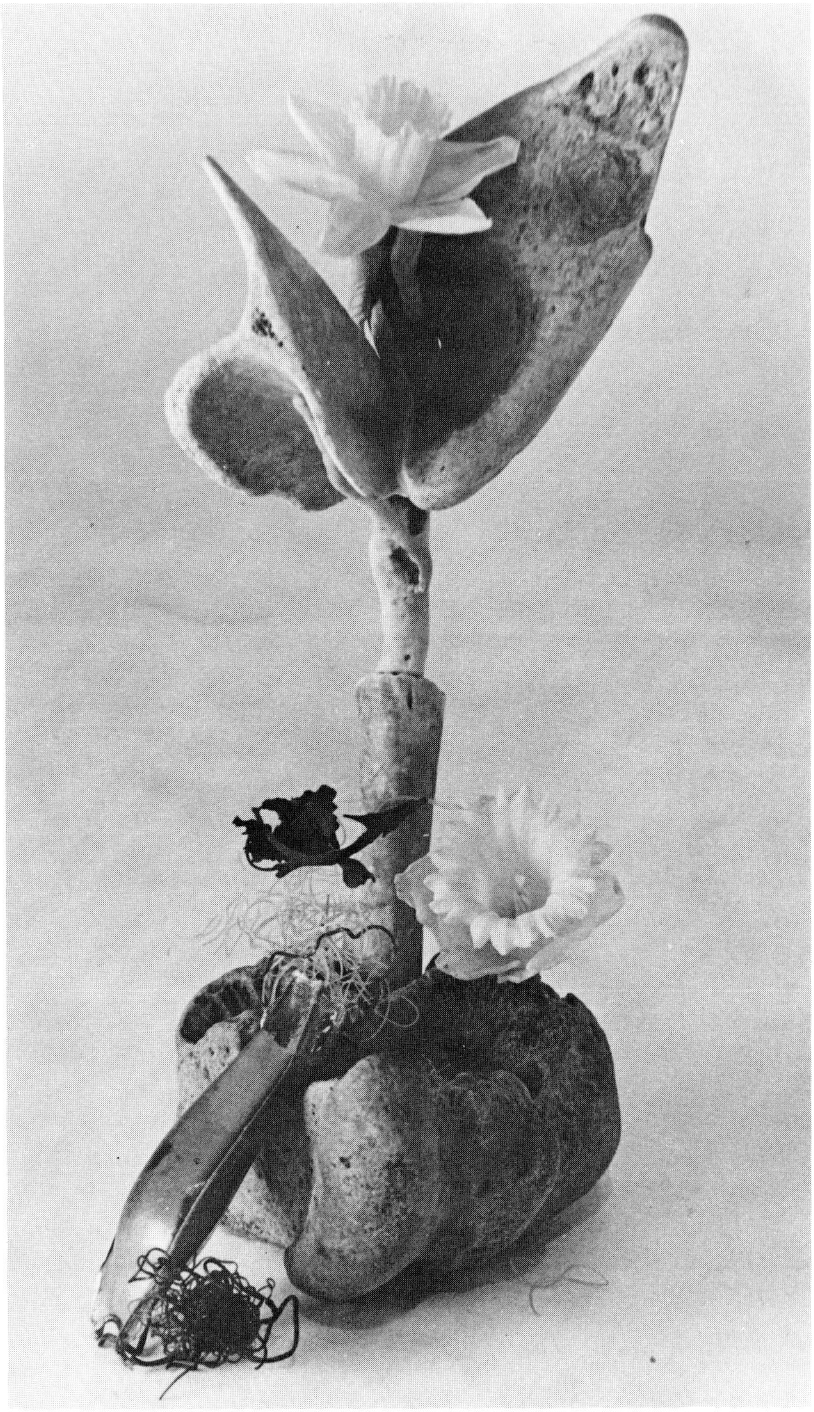

54 This sculpture, symbolizing flight and freedom, stands on a bone base enmeshed in nylon line and fragments of seaweed. A mermaid has paid tribute to the bird's passing by leaving her 'purse'. Two early spring daffodils are remembrance for a bird that no longer floats free on the wind. Nylon fishing line snared the bird's feet, and in its efforts to peck free its neck was caught, resulting in slow strangulation. The sculpture is entitled 'Epitaph to a Seabird' and the theme is 'Endangered Wildlife'.

Postscript : the driftwood magic

'People react to driftwood, and even more so to a driftwood sculpture.' If that phrase sounds familiar, it is; it was in the introduction. By now you will know how true it is, particularly if you have in the meantime collected driftwood and made a sculpture for yourself. If you have done so, you will also know how strange it is that something like this can make such a lasting impression. This book may soon be forgotten; interests can change and you might go for years without seeing any driftwood, but when and wherever it comes into your life again you will still have this feeling for it. As you hold it again in your hands you will sense its tranquillity touching you. It is an affinity that is difficult to describe, just an emotion which stirs quietly and pleasantly in the mind; when you feel this you will know that some of the magic has also rubbed off on to you.

Index